ONE LIFE TO LEAD

Russell Benaroya is an author and entrepreneur who began his career on Wall Street in investment banking and has since spanned multiple venture backed healthcare start-ups. Russell received his MBA from the Anderson School of Management at UCLA after a late 90s Internet blitz as Director of Corporate Development for Overture Services (acquired by Yahoo).

Russell speaks on topics designed to help entrepreneurs build more successful businesses. He is the host of a podcast called Stride 2 Freedom, where he helps business owners get and stay in their zone of genius. Russell has also done quite a bit of executive coaching for entrepreneurs around the concept of Entrepreneurial Endurance and that work (and his writing) are detailed on his personal website, www.thebenaroyagroup.com.

In the spirit of endurance, Russell not only has pushed him limits in business but also on the trail, as an ultra-trail runner with multiple 100 mile endurance runs.

Russell lives in Seattle with his wife, and two sons, Devon and Shane.

PRAISE FOR *ONE LIFE TO LEAD*

"With the pace of change, societal divisiveness, technological advances, and innumerable daily pulls on our time, it certainly can seem as if our lives are completely out of our control. In Russell Benaroya's timely book, *One Life to Lead,* he reminds us of the untapped and brilliant potential within each of our lives. Russell challenges us to clarify what matters most, embrace what we can influence, let go of all we can't, and be far more intentional in designing a life of true success. Read this book. Thank me later!"

—John O'Leary, #1 national bestselling author of *On Fire* and *In Awe*

"A successful life and career, I believe, require both an external and internal journey. In this book Russell shares his novel approach to designing both trips. The hard-earned insights captured in his five steps, reflect the humility it took to really get to know himself and the courage it required to translate his potential into action."

—Harry Strachan, former professor at Harvard Business School and director emeritus at Bain & Company

"As an investor in thousands of start-ups through Techstars, I've seen time and time again the difference that effective leadership can make in the entrepreneurial journey. *One Life to Lead* perfectly captures the essential but often unspoken ingredients necessary for great leadership in one's own life as a prerequisite to leading others."

—David Cohen, cofounder and chairman at Techstars

"Russell Benaroya has done the impossible here. He lays out a specific plan for how to design the life you want to live, the life you deserve to live—covering work, family, and relationships—with a simple-to-understand, comprehensive framework. He doesn't try to convince you by talking from on high, but rather by exposing his deepest vulnerabilities and sharing how not getting it right led to his own understanding and insight. Everyone can learn something important from this book, and I am going to start recommending it to people I care about tomorrow."

—Greg Gottesman, cofounder and managing director, Pioneer Square Labs

"With *One Life to Lead* Russell Benaroya helps us sidestep the oppressive and useless expectations many of us waste decades trying to exceed and move toward a path of curiosity, joy, humility, and purpose. He guides us to real success that we can feel and emanate. I could have used this book twenty years ago, and I am grateful for it now."

—Henry Albrecht, CEO, Limeade (a publicly traded global well-being company)

"The introduction of *One Life to Lead* gives us some important clues about what we are about to read. Russell Benaroya's vulnerability about his own life, both personal and professional, draws the reader in to want to learn more about what has worked, (and not worked) for him in his life. A major takeaway for me was to not compromise our core principles. They carry us to the success we all look for. His step by step approach on how to live a good life is straight forward and applicable for everyone."

—Greg Campbell author of *The Surprising Power of the Coil* and *The 5-2-1 Principle*, former EVP of Coldwell Banker

"Russell Benaroya is approaching superhuman status. There are few individuals in the world who come even close to combining Russell's unique mix of ultraendurance athlete, successful entrepreneur and CEO, author, and coach—all of which are integrated with his authentic care and appreciation for others. I try to learn from him as much as I can. In *One Life to Lead,* Russell distills real-world lessons into a plan that any leader can follow to design an ideal life and career. I especially recommend this book to anyone who is navigating a work-life transition. If this is you, read this book first! It will provide the foundation and insight to make your most important decisions with high confidence and wisdom. When you're at your best, doing what you are truly called to do, then you and your family benefit, your business benefits, and we all benefit. So invest in yourself by reading *One Life to Lead.* It is sure to pay priceless dividends for many years to come."

—Lex Sisney, author of *Organizational Physics* and *Designed to Scale*

"The pandemic. It conjures up thoughts and observations, insights and emotions. For me, I am increasingly observing how it has prompted many including myself to stop, take stock, and question what's next? Russell Benaroya has written a timely book that profiles entrepreneurs on their journeys of self-reflection through the lens of his five steps of life design.

Applicable not only to entrepreneurs, this model can be applied to corporate executives, nonprofit volunteers, and anyone who has hit the pause button to reflect on "what next".

—Deanna Oppenheimer, founder,
CameoWorks and BoardReady

"Russell has stepped into his genius zone in *One Life to Lead*. He has provided a road map for leaders to navigate their own ups and downs on the journey toward architecting great lives and successful organizations."

—Chris Winfield, cofounder of Super Connector
Media, entrepreneur and productivity wizard

"We do indeed only have ONE LIFE! I loved how Russell encapsulated insights from his own experience as well as the experiences of several others into an easy-to-follow framework and highly engaging book. It's a book that will deliver immense value every time you pick it up to read."

—Nitya Kirat, founder of YOSD Consulting
and author of *Winning Virtually*

ONE LIFE TO LEAD

Business Success Through Better Life Design

RUSSELL BENAROYA

RUPA

Published by
Rupa Publications India Pvt. Ltd 2024
7/16, Ansari Road, Daryaganj
New Delhi 110002

Sales centres:
Bengaluru Chennai
Hyderabad Jaipur Kathmandu
Kolkata Mumbai Prayagraj

Original English language edition published by Girl Friday Books
318 W Galer Street Suite 101, Seattle Washington 98119, USA.
Arranged via Licensor's Agent: DropCap Inc.

P-ISBN: 978-93-5702-805-9
E-ISBN: 978-93-5702-813-4

First impression 2024

10 9 8 7 6 5 4 3 2 1

Printed in India

For my wife and fellow adventurer, Melissa. We built a fence around our partnership to "design our life."

CONTENTS

FOREWORD

There comes a time in the life of individuals when it is appropriate to question—to reflect and search for purpose and meaning in their existence. This is particularly true of those who may have enjoyed some measure of success in their chosen profession or field. There is no end to the supply of books written by business leaders and entrepreneurs about their epiphanies as they try, in retrospect, to better understand their own journey and, of course, to provide prescriptions to others on how to design a more complete and fulfilling life.

The best reflections involve serious introspection and sometimes painful effort to confront the reality of one's existence. The quest to dig deeply into the organization of one's life—all of it—both personal and professional, takes lots of courage, humility, and self-confidence. To look inside of a life well lived is complex and not easy to do in a deep and thoughtful way. And then to think that your story, your lessons and insights, should be shared with the world is, well, presumptuous. Who are you anyway?

Meet Russell Benaroya.

Benaroya has undertaken the gruesome task of self-reflection and dared to risk a contribution to the goal of finding the balance between one's leadership in business and one's leadership of oneself. Like a deft sailor, he skillfully navigates the facts and stories that shroud his existence to allow us, as readers, a glimpse of the fundamental truths and principles that empowered him to design a new trajectory for his life.

The framework for life design is revealed over the ensuing pages in an easily understood and novel sequence of steps. Each step (cleverly laced with commentary from select interviews with influential people in his life called Designers), describes critical activities that anyone committed to getting unstuck should undertake. Step 1: *Ground Stories with Facts* and Step 2: *Establish Your Principles* set forth the initial condition for healthy design. Step 3: *Harness Energy from the Environment* and Step 4: *Get in and Stay in Your Genius Zone* elaborate on the resources and self-knowledge required in preparation for this journey. And Step 5: *Take Action* underscores the simple truth that no design can succeed without the courage to experiment and embrace new possibilities. Benaroya has proven this truth.

While Russell Benaroya is reflective in the way that he is choosing to manage his life, he is highly motivated and inspired to share his adventure with others. Each of us can make the choice to be more intentional in what we want out of our lives. His design framework resonates with concepts and themes I share with current students in my entrepreneurial strategy classes.

As human beings we can choose to take control and navigate our own life adventure. As Montesquieu noted, "It is always the adventurers who do great things." Benaroya has not disappointed. He has laid out an approach that you or I can follow.

Why do you want what you want? Learn to lead your one life and resolve to examine your own unfolding story with intentionality—now.

Alfred E. Osborne, Jr., PhD, Senior Associate Dean
Professor of Global Economics, Management, and Entrepreneurship
Faculty Director, Price Center for Entrepreneurship and Innovation
UCLA Anderson School of Management

WHY BUSINESS SUCCESS THROUGH LIFE DESIGN?

"Once everything works out for me professionally, *then* I'll turn my attention to other areas of my life." Right? Does that sound like something you have said before? Once you close one more deal. Once you raise a little more financing. Once you hire one more person. Once you improve profitability. Once you sell the company.

It sounds logical in some ways, to endure the struggle today for freedom tomorrow. We think, *Once I get there, then I'll have more time with my family, I'll strengthen my relationship with my spouse, I'll spend more time with my kids, I'll find a hobby. And, yes, I'll get in shape.* But there is a tragic flaw in that type of apparent logic: the very things you are putting off until you succeed are the ingredients necessary for success. In other words, success in life is not about business metrics. Rather, success in business is driven by your life metrics.

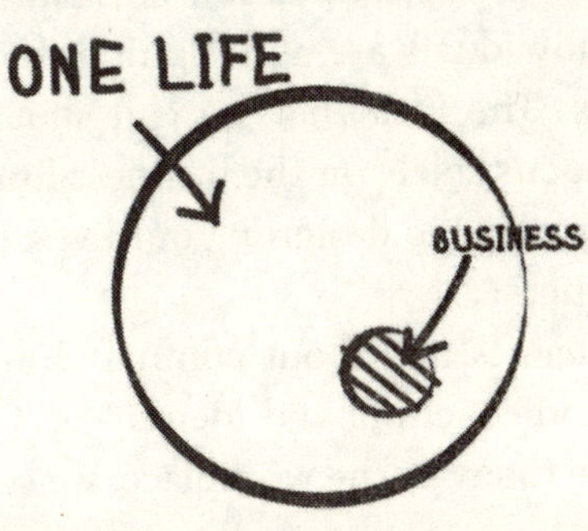

This is a book about driving business success, but it's not what you might think. It isn't about how to execute a business strategy or how to upgrade your team. It isn't about sales or marketing or improving efficiency. It isn't about how much money you might make. It isn't about how to lead others. It's about how to lead yourself.

When you realize that you have everything that you already need and that your business is a vessel for you to be your best self, your chances of success skyrocket. Why? Because you'll be able to see your blind spots without judgment or fear of failure. Your business doesn't predict whether you will be happy or unhappy in life. Whether it is going well or not doesn't reflect on who you are as a human being. Yes, your reasons for getting involved might be personal, and the underlying vision or purpose is sacred. But your role in the business, how the business functions, the risks, and the potentials are simply considerations to address, not existential decisions about who you are or what you will become. And that, my friend, is freedom.

If your business is viewed through the one-dimensional lens of making more and more money as the remedy for an internal struggle about your life, then it will be hard for you to lead others. You will lead out of a place of fear rather than a place of potential. You will feel stuck. I know, because there was a time when I felt stuck in that exact way.

Today, we are seeing an awakening. People are beginning to recognize that at the foundation of business leadership is how effective individuals are at designing their lives, not just their businesses. The idea that we can shut out everything around us and focus solely on the business limits our capacity to lead. If we can't lead in designing our lives, how are we supposed to lead others?

Leading others is not about command and control. It is about guiding and coaching and mentoring. Our authenticity radar is sensitive today in the workplace: we see right through individuals that lack self-awareness. The concept of work/life balance as some clear, bright line doesn't make sense anymore. In fact, work and life are not even separate. Life is life. Your business is a subset of that design, and your responsibility is to lead individuals on your team to be their best selves, both inside and outside of work.

Of course, there are people out there that seem successful in business but with an apparently unending ability to destroy everything else in their life except their business. But these are aberrations that rarely sustain in the long term. Eventually, these leaders—and typically their businesses and their lives—suffer.

That's not you, and if it were, you wouldn't have picked up this book. I understand the struggle, the tension between who you are, how you want to be, and how others want you to be. It is stressful. I finally changed my trajectory by prioritizing my life design and ultimately becoming a more conscious business leader. So can you!

INTRODUCTION

It was snowing. The kids were asleep in the back of the car. The Dalles is a gateway mountain range to the high desert of Central Oregon, and we were returning from a family trip. It was 2016, and Tony Robbins was schooling me on his podcast about the importance of intention. My wife, Melissa, and I were in a trance, watching as the snow got dismissed by the windshield wipers. We hadn't talked—really, really talked—in a long time. I had been running my start-up, and she had been raising the kids and getting her parent-coaching business going.

My feeling at the time was fear, fear that everything I had was hanging by threads, and at any moment, the bottom might fall out. I was angry, too. It was easier to be angry. My business partner and I were arguing. The business model we had designed wasn't unfolding as we had expected. My wife and I were not connected. I felt pressure to put on a front that everything was "great." I couldn't access my true feelings because they were buried under a mountain of blame. It was easier to look for reasons to rationalize the position I was in than it was to look in the mirror.

That Tony Robbins podcast was published in November of 2016 and titled "The 3 Steps to a Breakthrough." Of course it was. It was so Tony Robbins, the quintessential Tony Robbins, who reminds us that our greatest limitations are the ones we manifest between our own two ears. The message was as effective then as it is today. There was a place that I wanted to get to in my life, but I couldn't ever seem to make it happen. *OK, I'm interested,* said my inner voice. And there were a lot of reasons for that lack of progress. *Yes, tell me all of them, with answers, preferably, please. And I hope that my wife is picking up on this, too. She needs it.*

What became clear to me during that drive was that I didn't have a life strategy. I was moving, yes. I had action, yes. I had spent a lot of time thinking about and acting on the strategy in my business, but I never really thought about the strategy in my life. Why not? If I were a business, "Russell Benaroya, Inc.," what would my plan be? And yes, I have a business partner: my wife. Where is she in the plan? It annoyed me that I didn't have the answer. No, I was *angry* that I didn't have the answer. I was frustrated with my wife that we didn't have the answer.

I wanted to sound open and curious, but inside preferred to reach for blame. I asked my wife, "What is our strategy? We have never talked about where we want to be in five years." I asked it in a bit of a *Why haven't you ever thought of this?* tone, as if the responsibility for developing that strategy somehow wasn't mine to own. Her response was perfect. Not perfect in the sense that it validated my feelings, but perfect in the sense that it knocked me out of the story that I had been telling myself for years, a story that was not serving me, my family, or my life. She said, "Well, Russell, it has never been about us. It has always been about you and your business, and we've been along for the ride."

Fortunately, there was no ice on the road, because in that specific moment, I felt out of control. I realized how right she was and had been, but I couldn't admit it. I thrashed around in that conversation, trying to avoid taking responsibility for her statement, but it was pointless. She was right.

So, I did exactly what I thought I should do. I went online and found these great worksheets (I know, you have to be cringing a bit right now—I am, too) that are supposed to guide you through setting your future goals. I thought that what we had been missing was the tactical planning of where we wanted to be in five, ten, fifteen years. Oh boy. Melissa was a good sport about it, but like all the other times we'd tried that stuff, it fell flat. The worksheets never got referenced again, and only offered some short-term pain relief. The result? Failure!

That strategy failed because the problem had nothing to do with writing down goals and working toward them. The problem was so much more foundational for us. It was about breaking the habit of trying to rationalize our "righteousness" and getting real about the facts, our feelings, and how we could realign as partners—to learn if we even could realign as partners.

In that moment in 2016, on a small stretch of highway through the snow-covered pines of the Pacific Northwest, I realized that I was stuck. I had been building a life, but the structure felt shaky. I wanted a new design. I didn't know how to get it.

WHY ME?

For a long time, I thought I didn't deserve to write this book. I grew up in an upper-class household. I went to private schools, attended college, studied abroad, got a job on Wall Street, went to business school, worked in venture capital, got married, had two kids, and on and on. I was the center of my universe, and it was fine. There is nothing to complain about from the outside looking in, right?

I kept sailing, but I had no destination. In 2005 I made a shift to leave the safety of my career and start a company, confident (slightly overconfident) that I wouldn't be a statistic of start-up failure. It was the first time I ever really broke out of the mold of what I thought was expected of me. What I did not realize and had not planned for was that I was embarking on a fifteen-year odyssey of self-discovery, during which I would find myself swirling in a sea of uncertainty and self-doubt.

The easy thing would have been retreating back to the comfort of what is "expected," and that crossed my mind many times. The hard thing was looking at myself critically, knowing that I wanted to build a life on my terms but not being sure how to get out of my own way to do it. I constantly measured myself against what other people were doing professionally and where I stood in the pecking order. I had created an opportunity to design my life, but I didn't know how to walk through the door. My marriage was strained as we were living parallel lives while also raising two young children.

I had unconsciously committed myself to a life designed to look admirable, but it had a weak foundation. I felt held back by a series of blocks that were hard to see from the outside and easy for me not to acknowledge—until I had to. I was exhausted, and so was my family. Eventually, I began to shed the armor to get to the core of who I really wanted to be after years of justifying a certain way of being.

Eventually, I leapt.

WHY NOW?

In 2018, my family and I made a reasonably bold move and lived abroad for a year in San Jose, Costa Rica. We stepped out of the machine of what we "should" be doing and packed our bags to reboot our lives as a family, as professionals, and as a couple. And one day, sitting at a small table at a bakery called Picnic in Santa Ana, a little suburb of San Jose, I began to write. I came back the next day and wrote more, and before I knew it, I had found a groove and a path to expressing ideas and fears and frameworks that had been circling inside of me for years. It was like a dam of expression finally broke, where every keystroke poured out energy I had kept wrapped up for so long.

There were days I would write without a destination, but I had a lot bottled up that I wanted to express. It was emotional for me as I reflected on my decisions and the impact that those decisions had on people around me. I would end those days by looking up, slowly closing my computer, smiling, and feeling deeply grateful for the opportunity to be living in another country on this adventure with my family. I always felt a little lighter on those days, more confident in how I wanted to show up and move out into the world (well, in San Jose it was mostly into traffic) with ease.

It wasn't just my writing, either—everything changed. Melissa and I had summoned the courage to realize a dream we had since getting married: the desire to create an experience abroad as a family. We leapt and the world embraced us, opening our eyes to the possibility of possibility. Everything changed in that year abroad, personally and professionally. I started a new business that would give me the flexibility to work from anywhere in the world. I learned a new language. I made new friends. I reconnected with my family. I strengthened my partnership with my wife. And, yes, I wrote.

Finally, I was unblocking the obstacles that had been mounting for years. I was shedding the armor that was originally built to protect me but that was actually keeping out the positive energy I needed. I was able to see that my life was not so intimately tied to the business I was associated with; rather, my business could be tied to the life that I wanted to design. I saw that when I moved intentionally to make it happen in a way that worked for me, the universe would find ways to help me succeed. And it's why you can, too.

That's why I wrote this book, because the impediments to progress are self-constructed. When I finally realized that the things that I thought were happening *to* me were actually happening *by* me, I could take control and affect change.

WHY YOU?

Well, only you can answer that question, but I have spent time with hundreds of entrepreneurs and senior executives, listening to the circumstances they were letting drive their lives. The content keeps coming out faster and faster. These are "successful" people who spend time lamenting about their colleagues, their jobs, their spouses, their lack of finances, their health, the weather, their investors, their challenging customers, and their failed business deals.

Below the surface are the feelings that drive everything. Those feelings are anger, and frustration, and fear, and insecurity, and hope, and desire. Those feelings are hidden because most of us can't see (or don't want to see) that far underneath the surface to the root cause. But something doesn't feel right, something we can't articulate. We have covered ourselves in that protective armor. Now you are ready to shed it.

I want you to read this book because you have already read so many books on business leadership before, but you haven't seemed to crack the code. You know the frameworks. You know the case studies. You know the stories of those you admire. You know what you "should" be doing, but there is something inside of you that keeps wanting to convince you it's OK that you're stuck.

While you believe deeply in your potential, you have finally realized that you might be the greatest obstacle to unlocking it. You may read that sentence and find it makes no sense. No problem. You're not ready to read this book, and that's fine. Heck, it took me until I was in my thirties to start unpacking the feelings, thoughts, and behaviors that were influencing my career, my relationships, my unique gifts, and my limitations. And even then, it unfolded in pieces as new circumstances emerged that cast a harsh light on my greatest vulnerabilities.

This book is for the person who realizes that while we are the most liberated we have ever been, we create limitations to our freedom because we subscribe to society's desire for stability, things like a good job, a mortgage, good credit, flashy cars, and stuff. As we keep piling those things on, we slowly build a structure around ourselves that gives the illusion of stability but provides very little flexibility. The prospect of breaking out, taking a leap into the unknown, feels too risky. So we stay put. We end up trapped by a restrictive design of our own creation and by the expectations of others.

If that resonates, you're ready to read this book. You know that the path to success is yours to dictate, but you might not yet be sure how to build your life in a way to make it so. You are ready to let go of trying to control everything yourself, ready to begin listening and wondering and considering that what you don't know you don't know is exactly where you want to lean in. I want you to sit in that place, as uncomfortable as it is, and know that therein lies the learning that will help you unblock your potential. If you are ready to tap into the authentic you and to design your life, read this book. If you are ready to embrace that you have one life to lead, and you want to apply that learning to drive business success, read this book. If you are ready to make this a year of change you never thought possible, read this book.

This book is for the person who's tired of saying *I can't,* or *I never could imagine,* or *I wouldn't be able to,* and realizes that those are negative, self-spiraling narratives. We are all given the gift to reason and to make choices for ourselves. We are all given the ability to build and to create. But we have isolated ourselves into minuscule bubbles of self-importance, and then we blame the circumstances of life when we don't break out of them. No more.

HOW TO USE THIS BOOK

This book is a guide, broken down into steps that build on each other, called design steps. You may find that you're drawn to one area in particular because that is the part of your life that you want to architect, and that's great. There are many short stories in this book, written by a diverse group of business leaders that I have called Designers, who have shared part of their lives with you to amplify a principle. The book also has a series of exercises designed to help you unlock your own life design and look critically at the barriers that are holding you back.

ANYONE CAN DESIGN THEIR LIFE

Your life design is only limited by your imagination, and it requires that you take the first step, that you pose a fundamental question: Why do I want what I want?

It's a simple question, but don't intellectualize an answer. You answer it by how you choose to live your life. The goal of this book is not to script the answer to this question. This is a lighthouse question that will help keep you on course as you take the first steps in your intentional life design. Use this question as a reference point when you make decisions and take actions. *Why* you do something reveals a lot more than *what* you do.

I didn't start asking myself this question until I was firmly established in my career and had a family but still wasn't feeling successful. Why? Because life happens. We get stuck. I let it happen to me.

Designing your life requires a willingness to ask yourself questions about where you want to be and why, and then building a plan to get there. Without that road map, something is still going to happen. You may end up accidentally landing somewhere close to your idea of success, but it won't be intentional. It will be random, and the odds are not in your favor. Let's not leave it to chance.

THE PRIVILEGE OF THE WORK AHEAD

There is a great gift to be found in stepping back and observing how we have or have not designed our lives. Life design is an area of personal development that might seem overly theoretical, and in an environment where many of us are just trying to keep it together and meet our deadlines, it can seem like a luxury. The privilege is not lost on me, and the fact that you are reading this book imbues you with that same privilege.

Yet for a long time, I felt like I didn't deserve to do this work. My life was too busy, I told myself. I wasn't successful enough yet. This kind of work is reserved for people who have already achieved great things, I mistakenly thought. When you feel like you are in the theater of battle in your business, it feels ill timed to step back and assess the bigger strategy, lest you be taken out by the enemy. It's time to do battle, right?

I felt like that for a long time. Once I achieved a certain success (which I measured in dollars and accolades), I thought, then I would be able to get everything worked out. Do you understand the error of this? Once I achieve some desired outcome, only *then* will I start working on the ingredients to achieve a desired outcome? That is ridiculous thinking, and it's part of what kept me stuck for so long.

But let's go back to the question I posed earlier. We are all free to ask ourselves, "What do I want, and why do I want it?" While our means for action may feel limited, it is also worth noting that those feelings of constraint are often self-imposed, designed to keep us safe in what we know versus facing the uncertainty of the unknown. However, if you wait until you have achieved success to ask yourself this fundamental question of life design, then you've gotten it backward. Yes, timing matters, and we all traverse our own journeys with our own events and circumstances. But don't wait. Your trajectory will benefit from a well-designed foundation. So let's get to it.

THE FIVE STEPS OF LIFE DESIGN

"Freedom in this life is not money, and it's not success. The freedom of this life for me is having the ability to redesign it."

—Madeline Haydon, founder and CEO, nutpods

With all the thrashing that we do to figure out how we're going to make it in this world, the fundamentals of life design come down to five basic steps. These aren't prescriptions of what you will or will not accumulate in material possessions. Designing your life isn't so much about the car you want to drive, where you want to live, or how much money you want to make. Those are outcomes, and maybe they will unfold for you and maybe they won't. Life design is the framework for how you will lead.

The five steps of life design are:

1. Ground stories with **FACTS**.

   We have a tendency to tell ourselves stories that have very little to do with facts. As a result, we create a lot of drama and wind up feeling anxious, frustrated, and angry. Start with the facts first. We will discuss how to tell stories rooted in facts and how to harness stories that serve your life design.

2. Establish your **PRINCIPLES**.

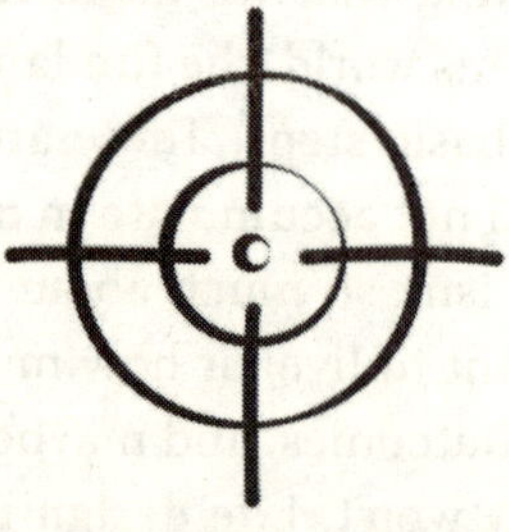

   Your principles represent a foundational code for how you want to conduct yourself in the world. They are the filters through which you make decisions, from day-to-day choices to your biggest, longest-term objectives. We will discuss how to identify and apply your own principles.

3. Harness **ENERGY** from the environment.

Energy is about putting yourself in an environment where you feel *energized*. The environment could be geographic. It could be an environment of people and relationships. You know where your energy is drained and where your energy is gained. Let's define it. Tap into it. And pursue it.

4. Get in and stay in your **GENIUS ZONE.**

Your genius zone is made up of the things you are uniquely qualified to do and how doing them causes you to lose track of time, to get into your flow state. You want to spend 80 percent of your time in your genius zone. We will discuss how to find your genius zone and how to live in it—as well as how to identify your anti-genius zone.

5. Take **ACTION.**

> Action is courage. Action is making a move toward your life design. It may be uncomfortable, but nothing was ever built by people standing around. We will talk about how to think about action and how to develop the courage you need to make things happen.

The steps here are intentionally simple, and they work in a sequence.

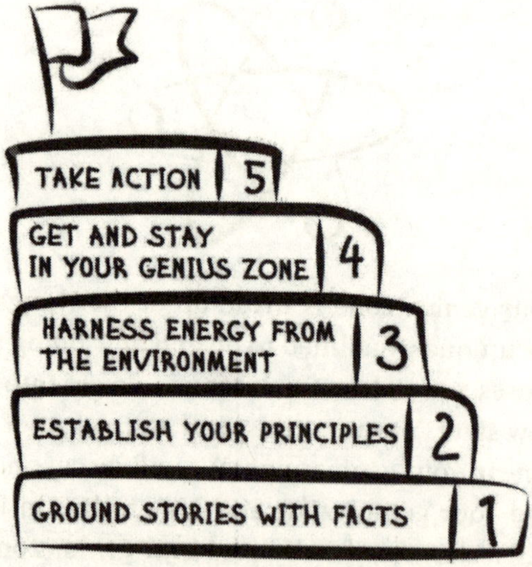

At the base, we uncover the barriers you have created through stories that have not served you (Step 1). We then move to setting your principles, which will give you more agency over your behavior (Step 2). Next, we create the environment where you feel your principles can best be lived (Step 3). Then, we focus on applying your time to those areas where you have a unique superpower (Step 4). Finally, we move to actualizing your design through discerning action (Step 5).

The work ahead is embedding these steps into the fabric of how you live your life, and how you lead. Once you grasp how these design principles apply to you, you will start to observe them in all kinds of different situations in your life and business. We can't predict the circumstances that will arise, but these design principles enable us to be grounded in how we approach them.

Once you ground your life design with these principles, how you apply them and what you do become less important. Why? Because you will be liberated to live a life of experimentation. Some things will work. Some things won't. Oh well. You will be able to apply the design to different scenarios without fear and see what happens. You'll be curious about it instead of fearful. In other words, your identity will no longer be cemented to what people see you do on the outside. Your identity (and your worth) will be driven by your own creation on the inside. Remember, it is your design, by design.

MEET THE DESIGNERS

I have the privilege of sharing firsthand stories to amplify the "one life to lead" design steps from some amazing individuals throughout this book. You will hear from people that are seemingly pretty successful, associated as they are with notable companies, strong businesses, and, in some cases, impressive educational pedigrees. Why did they choose to contribute, and why do I want you to know them?

I want you to know them not solely because of what they have built but because of their willingness to:

- Share their thirst for learning and self-discovery on their business leadership journey.
- Make business decisions grounded in principles of their life design.
- Demonstrate vulnerability in acknowledging their own limitations.

- Be seen as regular people leading with a purpose that isn't about material success.
- Take courageous action, even when the outcome is less than clear.

These individuals are just as prone to getting stuck as anyone. They face the same insecurities that many of us do around failure, fears that we aren't smart enough or that we aren't liked, uncertainty around our decisions, and feelings of being more lucky than skilled and of being abandoned or taken advantage of. But these are also individuals who aren't letting their fear hold them back.

Here is a brief introduction to the Designers, featuring the one piece of advice they would give their younger selves. You can read more about them in the Designer Professional Bios. While these individuals have all accomplished great things with their businesses, where they really shine is in sharing the aspects of life design that have contributed to and influenced their effectiveness in business leadership.

SARAH DUSEK

COFOUNDER AND FORMER CEO, UNDER CANVAS

www.undercanvas.com

"Asking yourself what it will take to achieve your goals opens the pathway of it happening."

Sarah is the cofounder of Under Canvas, a national glamping company committed to providing access to the outdoors. Sarah sold Under Canvas in 2018 for over $100 million and today is the founder of Enygma Ventures, a venture capital firm funding female entrepreneurs in Africa.

FRAN DUNAWAY

COFOUNDER AND CEO, TOMBOYX

www.tomboyx.com

"Don't rely on the perceptions of others to define who you are."

Fran cofounded a company to solve her fashion challenge and today has built a gender-neutral undergarments and apparel company that is empowering millions of people to be who they were born to be.

NICK SOMAN

FOUNDER AND CEO, DECENT

www.decent.com

"Earn your problems."

Nick cofounded Decent, an affordable and comprehensive insurance solution for small businesses to get health-care coverage.

MAX NELSON

FOUNDER AND CEO, HOOD

www.hoodhat.com

"All days are great. None are easy."

Max is the founder of an iconic apparel company that personalizes high-quality merino ball caps that represent the neighborhoods and communities that people identify with.

MATT OPPENHEIMER

COFOUNDER AND CEO, REMITLY

www.remitly.com

> "Get people around you that will ask you the right questions that will help you know yourself better."

Matt cofounded Remitly, an international mobile payments platform that was recently valued in excess of $1 billion.

MADELINE HAYDON

FOUNDER AND CEO, NUTPODS

www.nutpods.com

> "All the adversity, obstacles, disappointments, and, yes, pain that you will encounter will have a purpose. They will shape you."

Madeline Haydon founded the nondairy creamer company nutpods to solve her own problem. Today, as one of the most successful consumer product food companies on Amazon, nutpods has become an entrepreneurial success story (#13 in the Inc. 5000 fastest-growing companies in 2019) by an accidental entrepreneur.

KIRBY WINFIELD

GENERAL PARTNER, ASCEND VC

www.ascend.vc

"Run every day."

Kirby founded Ascend VC, a seed-stage venture fund in Seattle, after multiple public company exits. He invests in entrepreneurs at the beginning stages of their journey, when they are tackling their passions against all odds.

LORI TORRES

FOUNDER AND CEO, PARCEL PENDING

www.parcelpending.com

"Don't wait."

Lori built a smartlocker company for apartment buildings to better manage e-commerce shipments to residents. The company was sold in 2019 for over $100 million.

DAVID NILSSEN

COFOUNDER AND CEO, GUIDANT FINANCIAL

www.guidantfinancial.com

"If you're the smartest guy in the room and have all the answers, that's a big problem."

David's company unlocks retirement savings for thousands of small business owners to help them finance and grow their businesses. He has helped over twenty thousand entrepreneurs invest and manage over $4.5 billion to help them achieve their dreams.

SHARELLE KLAUS

FOUNDER AND CEO, DRY SODA COMPANY

www.drysoda.com

"Don't be afraid to ask for help."

Sharelle founded DRY Soda Company, a national beverage company that has revolutionized the dry cocktail movement.

JAMES MAYO

COFOUNDER AND CEO, SOS HYDRATE

www.soshydrate.com

"Run your own race."

James founded SOS Hydrate, a sports performance and beverage company. His inspiration came from his time in the military and his experience as a national running champion in the United Kingdom.

CASEY ROLOFF

FOUNDER AND CEO, SEABROOK

www.seabrookwa.com

"Travel to expand your mind."

Casey is the founder of Seabrook, a seaside town in Washington State that turned raw coastal land into a premier beach destination. He has built over seven hundred homes designed to create connections among individuals and the environment they inhabit.

GET INTO THE DESIGN MIND-SET

"Just create one street to start. Prove the concept, show people in a small space what is possible. Create that vision with that one street. Once people see it, it creates more creativity and collaboration about what the next street is going to look like."

–Casey Roloff, founder and CEO, Seabrook

Getting into the mind-set and having confidence that you are in control of your life design takes a little time. It's not a quick flip of the switch, especially if you have felt captive to things happening *to* you for most of your life. There are a few things to think about in preparation for embracing the steps of life design.

THE ONE QUESTION TO KEEP IN MIND: WHY DO YOU WANT WHAT YOU WANT?

We all have a quiet inner knowing that gets triggered when we are doing something and haven't fully decided whether it is what we want to be doing or where we want to be. It's easy to pack that feeling down, and we're especially good at it when it comes to business leadership, because the pressures to compromise for that next sale or partnership are strong, even if it runs counter to our life design principles. But don't ignore that inner voice. It is asking the most important questions.

"What kind of life do I want to have?"
—Madeline Haydon, founder and CEO, nutpods

So, I have two voices in my head. I think, A, because I'm a woman. I'm a female founder. I'm a person of color. I feel a pressure that I put up on myself to win when it is like, "Show the next generation of people, women founders, you know, women of color, that they can succeed in business." And then the other voice that I have is that quieter voice inside, which is like, "What do you want to do? Like, what kind of life do you want to have?"

The question that tends to get relegated to the end of the line is "*Why* do I want what I want?" Does saying what you want risk taking something away from someone else? Does it cut off other options and feel like it's committing you to something that might not be optimal? Is it hard to answer the "why" without being clichéd? Is the question simply too large and you don't yet know how to answer it?

We get so caught up in the "how" and the "when" of our want ("Well, how am I going to do that?" or "When will I ever find time to make this happen?") that we decide to not even to ask ourselves why and hope that everything just works out. Life design becomes a lot easier when we are intentionally pursuing what we want, underscored by knowing why. It is not designed to be an easy question to answer. The "why" might reveal itself at a very unexpected time, as you will see in Sarah's experience below. Once Sarah became aware of the question, she could get curious, and then start to plan, and, ultimately, take action. Her passion was investing in women. Today, Sarah is a social venture capitalist providing investment capital to female entrepreneurs in Africa.

"What will it take to make it happen?"
–Sarah Dusek, cofounder and former CEO, Under Canvas

One of the most profound questions I ever asked myself whilst building my business came from one of my mentors: "What do you really want?" It was a simple, powerful, and essential question. But until that moment in time I had never asked myself that question, ever. We had gotten into the groove of building the business, and we needed to keep putting more money in. The business had achieved a stage where we had an excellent team executing on the ground.

We had dreams and visions of doing other things and other passions, and it started to unleash creativity and a longing to make those things happen, and so we started to ask ourselves what it would take to make that happen. We stepped back and realized we had a target number in mind for selling the business. I had a dream about becoming an investor myself and investing in other women.

When I realized what our number was and we worked backward from that number and figured out what it would take to make that happen, it certainly was not as far out of reach as I thought. It wasn't even five years away. Instead it could have been one year away. After realizing what I really wanted, I got really disciplined. This is the goal–*I'm going to make that happen*, and I did. We sold the business for that number by the end of that year. Knowing what you really want creates a pathway to making it happen.

I deflected the question myself for a long time, and probably still do in certain areas of my life. Why? Because when you express what you want, you are also implying what you *don't* want, and that can be scary. It may impact your relationships. It may take you down a different path from the one you've been on for the past several years. But it will also give you great strength. It will make your life design a lot simpler, because you aren't trying to keep all your options open anymore. You are stating an unequivocal desire that no one can take away from you. How the world responds is not for you to try to control.

FUTURECASTING: A STRATEGY FOR EXPRESSING YOUR WANT

Every year, my wife, kids, and I get together on New Year's Day to reflect on the past year and write down our intentions for the upcoming year. I have a reputation for being "all business" or "AB," so my approach doesn't always get a warm reception. We get through it, I feel good that we did it, and all the stuff that we wrote down? Well, we dust it off at the end of the year and look at it. It was never alive. It didn't get embedded into our practice as a family. In other words, it was a wasted opportunity. Futurecasting presents a better way.

Futurecasting is the act of projecting where you will be in the future as if it has already happened. Because the future resides entirely in our minds, planting the seeds of how we want it to unfold will significantly increase the likelihood of it happening. This is not just about unfolding toward an outcome, either. It is just as much about futurecasting how you behaved, how you treated yourself and others, and how you managed conflict along the way. It is just as much about how you showed up as it is about the points you put on the board. With futurecasting, you can begin to work backward and determine what you want to be doing today so that you can actualize your story by the end of the year.

Futurecasting is shifting from "I will" to "I did." You are transporting yourself into the future to recount your last X months or years. Approach it holistically—don't limit it to work or friends or family. Let it just flow. Get it out there.

Exercise: Futurecasting

- You can do this exercise in a journal or on your computer.
- Try to look out for at least twelve months.
- Think about someone you are close to (a close family member or friend) and where you want to be seen more authentically by them.
- Structure your futurecast in the form of a letter where you aren't just recounting what happened but trying to help people close to you feel what you are feeling. Don't shy away from this vulnerability.
- Make it real. Write deeply. Make it a story. Bring us into the moment a bit more.
- Key reminders:
  - This is less about whether or not things worked out exactly as you wrote them down (note: it gets a lot hazier the further out in time you write), but more about how you approached your life, how you designed it.
  - Designing your life isn't about the exact results but rather about the way you choose to show up in the world.
- Bonus points: Consider reaching out to the person you wrote this letter to and asking if you could share it with them.

You don't always have to futurecast to get to work on the principles of life design, but it is helpful to answer the "why" of your actions and decisions. Futurecasting creates that stronger "why." Now that you have futurecast, you have a clearer path and purpose for exercising the Five Steps of Life Design.

THINK IN TERMS OF EXPERIMENTS

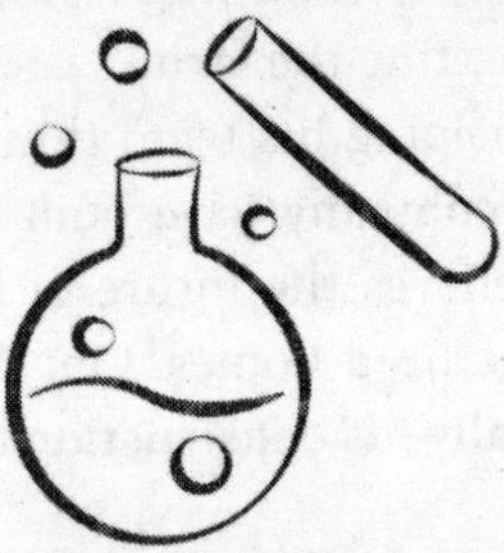

Any big idea or shift in our behaviors or actions can feel overwhelming. In fact, sometimes it can be so overwhelming that we decide not to even bother going for it. We don't want to fail. It is easier to play it safe. It is easier to manage what we know than to approach the unknown. And it is exactly that "play it safe" approach that gets us stuck every time. That's why "experiment thinking" is much more approachable.

Carol Dweck pioneered the research around growth versus fixed mind-sets in her groundbreaking book, *Mindset: The New Psychology of Success*. Dweck's work demonstrates the value of thinking in terms of experiments. She suggests that those with a fixed mind-set believe their intelligence is static, so they try to look smart with what they have; they avoid challenges, criticism, effort, and obstacles—they avoid experimenting. Those with growth mind-sets, on the other hand, embrace the concept that our learning and intelligence are to be developed; therefore, they embrace challenges, persist in the face of setbacks, and learn from criticism and failure. People who cultivate growth mind-sets are better able to shift their perspective and get unstuck.

Thinking in terms of experiments paves the way to move from a fixed to a growth mind-set. Thinking experimentally means taking small actions that begin to change your belief systems, being open to an outcome without presupposing what the outcome is going to be. It is about making small shifts in your identity and behavior, learning from those shifts, and not feeling like you are betting the farm.

Casey Roloff is helping his team think in terms of experiments. He and his company have built over seven hundred homes. Today, he believes the future of housing could be in reimagining manufactured homes. Oh, the heresy! His team was resistant, especially his construction team.

"It doesn't come with a steering wheel."
–Casey Roloff, founder and CEO, Seabrook

I definitely approach taking chances or taking risks by starting very simply, making a low-risk decision and verifying the proof of concept. This morning is a great example. I am talking to my leadership team about manufactured homes, and my construction guy is giving me the hardest time, asking if it's going to come with a steering wheel.

I'm enjoying the bantering, but it's really all about education. I want my team to be fully educated before making a final decision. I've taken the time to be educated. I've seen the product. I've walked the factory. And, you know, I'm very confident about this. And I want my team to become as confident as I am about this. And if they see something along the way that is a pitfall, bring it up. I'm not going to commit until I get the wisdom of the group around me to tear it apart so we can learn together.

Life design is about conducting a lot of little experiments when you are equipped with and exercising the Five Steps of Life Design. Some experiments will work out and some won't—that's the whole point. But 100 percent of the time, the intent is to learn from these experiments. Experiment thinking is growth mind-set thinking, and it has a way of making potentially scary changes feel less intimidating.

GRASP THE DIFFERENCE BETWEEN GOALS AND INTENTIONS

In 2015, a study by psychologist Gail Matthews showed that when people wrote down their goals, they were 33 percent more likely to achieve them. I'm not interested in convincing you that you should set goals. We already know they matter. I also don't want to belabor the difference between goals and intentions except to say this: goals tend to be very binary (you either did it or you failed) and can have unintended consequences if you're not successful. For example, if you are rewarded when you achieve goals and punished when you don't, two things might happen. First, you probably aren't going to set any more goals that seem risky. Second, you aren't going to be as comfortable sharing your goals, even though we know it is a proven way to increase your odds of success.

So instead, I tend to talk in terms of intentions. Intentions are more about the things that I do, that I can control, that are consistent with how I want to live my life intrinsically (my principles), and that I believe will result in achieving a goal. Think of intentions as the inputs and the goal as the output. I have an intention to write five hundred words per day. My goal is to publish a book. I have an intention to live a life of adventure. I have a goal to climb Mount Kilimanjaro. I have an intention to set aside special one-on-one time with my kids. My goal is to have a relationship with my children that transitions to a friendship as they get older.

As you can see, intentions and goals go hand in hand. It is hard to set an intention without knowing what it is in service to. This book is primarily about intentions, meaning that life design is largely in your control. You get to decide. What is so exciting about a life design framework is that once the foundation is established, you will be more nimble naming your intentions (inputs), such that your goals (outputs) will be easier to accomplish. Why? Because the underlying requirements to achieve your goal will already have been established, and those requirements are inside of you: namely, living your intentions. Life design makes achieving your goals much more possible.

BE A LUCKY PERSON

One of the biggest looming insecurities I've found in my hundreds of conversations with business owners is the fear that they are more lucky than good. And the truth is, they're probably right—but that's a good thing! Luck is not an aberration or some unknowable cosmic force. In fact, being lucky is a core feature of the life design mind-set. Gay Hendricks and Carol Kline in *Conscious Luck* offer a simple but profound message: by simply identifying ourselves as lucky and making the conscious decision to be a lucky person, we will create circumstances in our lives that seem lucky.

I know this to be true, because it happened to us when we moved abroad, to Costa Rica. Once we were clear on what we wanted in pursuit of our year abroad (our intention), some incredible things started happening. We found ourselves introduced to some amazing people in San Jose who brought us in to help make our transition easy (even letting us spend the night at their house and leave our bags with them as we got settled). We met people randomly while in Costa Rica and learned that we had mutual friends in the United States. I was invited to work on a project with an investor in Costa Rica. I ended up buying a business and starting a new career.

We consistently felt lucky and welcomed that luck into our life versus dismissing it as a fluke and preparing for the other shoe to drop. "When you are clear on intention, the universe can do its work," I like to say. It knows how to help you. When you aren't clear, the universe doesn't know how to help you. In *Conscious Luck*, Gay and Carol talk about how, by releasing our personal barriers, we open ourselves up to good fortune. You are already a lucky person.

Expanding your luck is a state of mind. You can choose how you look at setbacks. Will you embrace them and acknowledge they are there to help you in some way, or will you resist them and fight back because you believe you are entitled to getting what you expect? If you affirm that you are a lucky person, you will reap great value.

"Lean into the doors that are open."
–Max Nelson, founder and CEO, HOOD

When I finally stopped trying to bang down the doors that were closed and lean into the doors that were open, things started to improve for me. I began to look at rejection as protection. It is as it is supposed to be. For the entrepreneur, there is this expectation that we're supposed to do whatever it takes, that celebrities need to wear my hats, and they need to get photographed so it can go viral as quickly as possible. I'm not saying that I'm not aggressive, but I'm clear on why I'm doing HOOD. The company is aligned with my belief systems. One is an extreme commitment to service, and the other is a patience that everything will unfold exactly as it should, when it should. I don't know what it's going to be exactly, but every day, something happens.

I have a process orientation, not a results orientation. I made hats for LeBron James and his son. I haven't seen either of them wearing them yet, and that's fine. Maybe they didn't fit well or they gifted them to someone else. Who knows? That's not my business. My business is making the best hats out there that I can.

GET INTO THE DESIGN MIND-SET
CHAPTER SUMMARY

The design mind-set is about making a commitment to viewing your life as something that is moldable and in your control, not dictated by others. Here are the highlights:

- The most important question to ask yourself is "Why do I want what I want?" It may take time for the answer to unfold, but without keeping that question top of mind, life design is difficult.
- Futurecasting is an effective way to forecast your life in a way that is less about bullet points and more about recounting it as if it already happened.
- The actions you take in life design are about conducting a lot of little experiments. Experiments are the learning modules that provide feedback on your design. Experiments are also less daunting.
- Intentions are the inputs. Goals are the outputs. Intentions tend to be more in your control, whereas the outcome may or may not unfold as you have planned. Intentions and goals are both important in life design, but recognize the distinction.
- You are a lucky person. Your luck is amplified when you are clear on the commitments that you are making.

GET INTO THE DESIGN MIND-SET
CHAPTER SUMMARY

The Exercise in This Chapter

- Futurecasting

Highlighted Designers

- "What kind of life do I want to have?"
—Madeline Haydon
- "What will it take to make it happen?"
—Sarah Dusek
- "It doesn't come with a steering wheel."
—Casey Roloff
- "Lean into the doors that are open."
—Max Nelson

STEP 1: GROUND STORIES WITH FACTS

"One of the things that I've really been examining are the stories that I have about myself, and those that no longer serve me."

–Madeline Haydon, nutpods

Everything that you think might happen from this second onward is a story. The future has not come to pass. However, we live most of our lives telling ourselves stories about the future that aren't grounded in reality. They are grounded in our *perception* of reality, which may or may not have data to support it. And, unfortunately, many of the stories we tell aren't helping us move forward. Instead, they're creating barriers that affect our ability to ask the right questions and identify the right problems. I don't know if I am going to lose that deal. I don't know if I'm going to run out of money. I don't know if my employee is going to leave. I don't know if I'll be able to resolve that conflict with my parents. I simply don't know. And any reference to that unknown as a fact is simply not true.

The fact that we can even imagine a future is what makes humans so incredibly remarkable. Yuval Noah Harari, in *Sapiens*, asserts that it is our ability to create and believe fiction that has kept us alive. We have a unique ability to create new fictional realities, and that creativity is our primary survival mechanism. At a large scale, fictional realities like heaven, money, and corporations are designed for broad cooperation. But at an individual level, our fictional realities about our place in the world can sabotage our life design.

What are the clues that you are creating a fictional reality? When you ask questions or make statements like these:

> "What will people think?"
>
> "I could never do that."
>
> "If we do that, then this other bad thing is going to happen."
>
> "I'm not good enough."
>
> "That sounds too risky."
>
> "We will never be able to achieve these goals."

All these statements are about some imagined reality that hasn't even happened yet. However, the more you believe in your imagined reality, the more likely it will turn into objective reality, because your mind-set becomes predisposed to that outcome, and it is an outcome that won't serve your life design. It's not what a lucky person would do. We also tend to take this imagined reality, assume it is fact, and then adapt our lifestyle to fight against it instead of building the life we really want.

Business leaders often fail to ground their stories in facts. Drama in the workplace is typically a symptom of this very issue. When we have conflict around stories that aren't grounded in facts, it's often the loudest voice, or the squeaky wheel, that will prevail. And that's a suboptimal outcome. In 2009 I was in the office of one of my investors, and my business partner and I shared that we would be leaving the company that had recently acquired us. For reasons that probably require that I write another book, this investor became enraged and threw us out of his office. That event haunted me for a number of years because I was willing to let his story become the truth, until I finally figured out that his reaction had everything to do with *his* story, not the facts.

Brené Brown, famously known for her multimillion-view TED Talk, has become a leading voice on shame and vulnerability. In books like her bestseller *Rising Strong*, she reminds us that the most dangerous stories we tell ourselves are usually about our worthiness. Her research focused on the stories people told themselves about lacking lovability after a breakup, divorce, or an uncaring relationship with a family member. But it is equally present in business.

If we bring that same need to prove our worthiness into how we lead our business, we are going to spend more time hustling for validation than focusing on the best decisions for the business, even if they aren't the most popular. You cannot tell yourself shame-based stories in your life and expect to insulate yourself from that mind-set when you lead your business.

"We all have our fear-based stories."
–Sharelle Klaus, founder and CEO, DRY Soda Company

When I started DRY Soda I thought I could do no wrong for the first five to six years. I was so committed to being right, but inside of me was this insecurity that I didn't go to a great undergraduate school and people would think that I wasn't capable of leading this company. I didn't have an MBA. CEOs don't make mistakes. A real CEO would know what to do. I would say these things in my head. And then I had this epiphany, about seven to eight years into running the company, where I was at a board meeting and there was a woman on my board and she was tough, someone that kind of scared me. I had tried a marketing campaign that didn't work, and she said, "OK, well, that didn't work, so what's the next thing to try? What did you learn from it?"

And it dawned on me in that moment that I was running my company in a fear-based way because of the stories I was telling myself about where a CEO should come from and what they should know how to do. I was so scared to make mistakes because of what I thought other people would think that I was wound up all the time, and that stressed out everyone around me.

I finally had the chance to step back and enjoy a sigh of relief when I talked to a couple of other beverage CEOs who shared their experience. I remember this one guy, Seth Goldman, who just started laughing when I recounted the ways that I had been leading from a place of fear, and he said, "Sharelle, I have made so many mistakes. I have made them all." And I'm like, *Oh, Mr. Perfect Seth has made so many mistakes! What a relief.*

Our stories typically come from a place of fear, and that fear is built to protect us (it's the whole "not wanting to get eaten by a lion" thing). What *might* happen can be paralyzing because we only know what we know. We know the safety of our surroundings. We tell a story about the unknown being more risky or less satisfying than the current situation, when in reality, the world is much bigger than our little snow globe.

WHAT'S A FACT?

It is not always easy to distinguish a story from a fact (modern-day media can attest to that). A fact is something that is indisputable, something that you could record with a video camera. This might sound obvious, but in a charged situation where you feel an emotional connection to the situation (circumstances at work, or with your spouse, your parents, etc.), it is surprisingly easy to confuse stories for facts. Examples of facts include:

- Someone spoke words aloud.
- When this person spoke, their voice was raised.
- She reacted with a curled-up lip and a furrowed brow.
- We achieved X percent of our target goal for the quarter.
- The sun is shining.

Facts are swirling all around us, but the truth is, facts are kind of boring. We thrive on what is underneath the facts, what we think is being implied by the facts—and that emotional interpretation is what we react to. Our entire civilization is based on the power of storytelling. Stories are in our blood, and they are the vessels that connect the passage of time and foretell the possible future. But stories are told through the lens of the storyteller. I suppose that is why you can watch Fox News and CNN discuss the same set of facts but get a very different story.

Next time you are watching the news, or sitting in a meeting, or having a conversation with someone, listen intently for the facts. You may find it quite enlightening how little factual information is conveyed. Building your fact radar is powerful and breaks through so much unnecessary content that really has no material impact on you (unless you let it).

Stories often get conjured up in reaction to the statements or actions of others. As we will discuss later, when we lack clear principles for our conduct, we become vulnerable to the stories others tell. If we're not careful, we assume those stories are objective facts (even if you can't record them with a video camera, for example), and that assumption can spiral in negative ways.

THE UNARGUABLE POWER OF FEELINGS AS FACTS

Let me twist the definition of facts just a little bit by introducing the unarguable power of feelings as facts. When something occurs, I have some emotional reaction that is driven by how I am perceiving it (my story). I might feel sad or anxious or excited or overwhelmed or frustrated. These are also facts but in a different way. They are unarguable truths. They aren't measurable by someone else, but they are mine to own. No one can tell me that I "shouldn't feel this way." I don't need to justify myself, because I can't help how I feel. I am who I am. Accepting your feelings is the gift that comes from acknowledging that stories are subjective.

Stories create feelings, and it's feelings that we wrestle with most often. The story that we create is what drives some emotion. There is nothing emotional at all about a fact. It happened. There is no meaning to it until we apply a meaning and then, when we apply a meaning (our story), it conjures up some emotion, and it is that very emotion that we grapple with. If we can tap into that emotion by expressing it and talking about it (versus the content of the story itself), it is going to be a lot easier to move through your life and lead your business with less consternation. Why? Because you are in control to do the work yourself to understand your emotion versus trying to compete with someone else about why you think your story is right. It is much easier to resolve issues easily when you can express that you're feeling anxious versus explaining why you think they are wrong.

Here is a scenario to explain the point: I have a colleague who consistently misses deadlines (fact), and I feel super-frustrated (fact) because I miss my deadlines (fact) and that poorly reflects on our organization (story). My colleague does not understand just how much of a problem she is creating (story), and that puts our business in jeopardy (story).

Here is the strategy for dissecting that scenario into something that can be acted on productively. The facts are that I have a colleague who misses deadlines, I miss my deadlines, and I'm frustrated. That's it. Everything else makes certain assumptions that might not be true but further entrench me in a set of beliefs that aren't serving me or the organization. What I need to do is be able to express my frustration and own that emotion. My colleague is not "making me feel frustrated."

I am. Now I'm a lot more equipped to speak with my colleague, own my emotion, and see if we can find a shared path forward without creating an overly contentious situation.

Just to realize that you are in control is a major learning edge breakthrough in life design. Now you can spend less time spinning up on every circumstance in your life that tends to create unnecessary drama and isolate the work to unpacking and resolving why you have that feeling (a feeling that probably emerges in many more situations beyond just your colleague missing deadlines).

The critical link here of owning my feelings was a breakthrough in my life design journey. And while I had a lot of work to do if I wanted to become a better business leader, the place to do the work needed to begin in my personal life.

"That's not a feeling. That's a backhanded criticism."

—Russell Benaroya

In 2017, Melissa and I were drifting apart, could not agree on my next career move, were running parallel lives, and were faced with figuring out "Where do we go from here?" We agreed to do a two-day intensive retreat with Phil, a business coach I had been working with for a while.

One of our biggest challenges was that when we argued, we argued about the situation. For example, we argued about me starting a new business, or Melissa trying to build her online business, or me not being around enough. Phil told us to think of that as the wrapping paper. But beneath the wrapping paper, inside the box, is the real issue. Inside the box are the feelings that drove the thoughts that drove the actions that resulted in the conflict. So it would stand to reason that if we began with the feeling and attended to that, maybe we could understand why the conflict arose in the first place.

I was happy to begin. "I feel that you don't understand why I need to travel as much as I do."

Phil cut me off abruptly. "That's not a feeling. That is a backhanded way of criticizing Melissa."

Oops. Darn. But it felt so good to be right! It was hard for me to access my true feelings. He reminded me that feelings are things like anger, joy, frustration, concern, exhaustion, judgment, insecurity, fear, etc.

Melissa was much better at it. She said, "I feel unsafe because I don't know our plan to build security, and so I react when things arise that make me feel unsafe."

I said, "I feel judged because I don't believe I am living up to your expectations, and I am stressed because I'm not sure how to get there."

It was such a powerful exercise because it wasn't about Melissa doing something to me. It was about me reacting to a set of actions in a particular way. I could lean into safety, and Melissa could lean into judgment. I didn't want her to feel unsafe. She didn't want me to feel judged. We talked about ways we could help her feel safer and about ways that I could navigate without the feeling of judgment. It was a step in the right direction.

From there, we could build a foundation. Armed with some new tools, especially the tool of leading with feelings, we had a pretty successful month before we headed back to see our coach for a check-in. We were in the zone of talking more about the life that we could create together. It felt good.

Exercise: How to Separate Fact from Story

- Think of a situation or circumstance in your life that you feel is dragging you down.
- Write down the facts of the situation. Be sure to only include the actual facts—things anyone could look at and agree with, without interpretation. One measure to use is whether these could be filmed.
- Now write down the whole sordid story—everything about the situation as you perceive it and how it impacts your life.
- Write down the feelings that the story conjures up for you.
- Look at the amount of facts you wrote in comparison to the story you told. Generally, there will be far fewer facts and a whole long, sordid story.
- Now, consider yourself lucky that you could tease apart fact from story, and get curious why those stories exist for you.
- If that situation involves another person, as it usually does, now you can reach out to them with the ability to own your story and your feelings and share what you would like to see happen. Then let them do the same thing. The opportunity for resolution will be much greater.

The "fact" is that there are usually a limited number of facts in any situation. The story dominates how many of us navigate our world and how we perceive ourselves.

THE POWER OF BELIEF BUBBLES

If stories are all just made up, why not tell stories that build you up instead of tear you down?

One of my coaches, Lex Sisney, shared a concept with me called belief bubbles. I had called him in 2014 from a conference room at the company I was CEO of at the time. I had received some bad news. The company I had sold my start-up to in 2009 had abruptly closed its doors, and all the ownership my investors had in that business vanished. It wasn't an orderly closing of doors, either—this company literally put a sign on the door that it was done. It made me sad because it was a health-care business with many patients who needed to be served. I was angry and disappointed but not totally surprised, given the dubious leadership of the company. What hurt the most was that the failure of the company had also been my own, in the story I was telling. I couldn't see the situation clearly.

Here is what helped: Lex asked me to turn off the lights and close my eyes. *OK, this is weird,* I thought. He asked me to consider the following:

1. Imagine being surrounded by bubbles, and within those bubbles are all the stories associated with the simple fact that this company shut its doors.

2. Look at the bubbles as they are passing by, and just watch them.
3. Let the bubbles pass by that told the stories that:
    a. I should have known better.
    b. I had responsibility for the demise of a company five years after I sold it.
    c. I am a failure because the company failed.

He then asked me to look at the bubbles that contained the following:

1. I exited a company during a recession, based on the best information that I had at the time.
2. I acted on the best opportunity we had to sell the company to this buyer. Using the knowledge we had, we thought that it would be a stable platform to continue growing and create equity value.

How about those bubbles? Are they any less true? Yes, it was unfortunate that the company did not continue on as I had hoped, but the only facts were that I sold the company and the company that acquired it shut down.

I had a choice to grab on to one belief bubble while letting others just pass by. The belief bubble I grabbed was up to me. Why grab one that painted a picture that drained my energy, created self-doubt, and devalued my worth? Untangling from a default state of mind that insists, "When shit goes wrong it is a reflection on my worth" takes a *lot* of work. Belief bubbles are one cool strategy for reframing your perspective.

Here's how the "It's a 'get to'" belief bubble came into my life and why it's so powerful . . .

"It's a 'get to.'"
–Russell Benaroya

In 2011, I had just completed TechStars Seattle, a well-known mentorship-driven technology accelerator designed to help increase the probability of business success. The program takes a select group of founders/leaders and sequesters them for three months in a highly intensive program supported by mentors and peers. It was a grueling three months, but so rewarding. The business my partner and I were building was a "mileage rewards plan for health." We had the support of a health insurer and were ready to raise capital and grow the team.

Three weeks after the TechStars program ended, I was served with a lawsuit from the organization that had acquired my last company just a few years prior. I was no longer involved with that business, so I was rattled in a big way. The lawsuit alleged that I had breached a term of the acquisition agreement–and to make things even more exciting, every single one of my shareholders was served with the lawsuit as well. I was floored and freaked out. The allegation was petty and frivolous, as it turned out. The company was using the lawsuit as a tactic to get a shareholder to back off from some aggressive behavior.

I was coming into one of the most exciting times in my life and . . . BAM! I worried the reputation I'd worked so hard to build was going to be torpedoed. What would people think? I sat down with my friend and mentor Andy Sack, who listened to me fret about my current situation.

His response? "Wow, Russell, this sounds like a 'get to.'"

"A what?" I asked.

"A 'get to,'" he said. "Think about it: this is a unique experience for you. No one is going to die from this. So few people get to go through this. See what you can learn through this process. You get to go through it."

I had never thought about a "get to" before, but it made so much sense. I can choose to fear, or I can choose to be curious and learn. The same facts were in play, but the "get to" put a totally different application on the situation. That alone took some pressure off of me. It helped me see that this wasn't really about me at all, but that I was being used as a vehicle by the other side to get closer to their own goals. Instead of stewing in my fear and anxiety, I was able to get the situation resolved quickly and moved on with the exciting opportunities in front of me. Yes, it was challenging, but Andy was right: no one died.

Exercise: Belief Bubbles

1. Think of an unresolved situation you have struggled with in your past, either personally or professionally.
2. Write down the facts of the situation. Focus on the snapshot-worthy facts.
3. Write down the beliefs you have held about it. Oftentimes, the beliefs will be around what happened to you or what someone did to make you feel a certain way.
4. Close your eyes for two minutes and visualize those stories captured in bubbles, and watch them pass you by. Don't try to grab them. Just let them pass. Now open your eyes.
5. Write down a different story, one that gives you energy or contemplation or calm, one that is equally as believable as the story you released.
6. Close your eyes for one minute. See that story in a belief bubble, and rather than letting it pass you by, grab it. Bring it inside you. Let it fill you up.

Is the new story as believable as the one that caused you so much frustration and angst? Does it make you feel more open, calm, or confident? Does it reduce some of your fear?

Simply going through this exercise can create some space for you to look at a situation from a different perspective and be a little less hard on yourself. Part of life design is putting yourself in control of your stories.

GROUND STORIES WITH FACTS
CHAPTER SUMMARY

We covered some good ground in this chapter and set the tone for the rest of the book. So much of our life is about manufacturing stories from a small number of observable facts. Here are the key takeaways:

- Facts are indisputable. Everyone will observe the same thing.
- Most of our angst and challenge comes from the stories that we create from a small set of facts.
- Often, those stories are in our heads and not meant to build us up, but are driven by our fears.
- Underneath the stories are our feelings, and those feelings are unarguable if you own them without blaming others.
- You control the belief bubbles, the stories that you tell yourself.
- Getting in control of your stories is a fundamental premise of life design.

GROUND STORIES WITH FACTS
CHAPTER SUMMARY

Exercises in This Chapter

- How to Separate Fact from Story
- Belief Bubbles

Highlighted Designers

- "We all have our fear-based stories."
  —Sharelle Klaus
- "That's not a feeling. That's a backhanded criticism."
  —Russell Benaroya
- "It's a 'get to.'"
  —Russell Benaroya

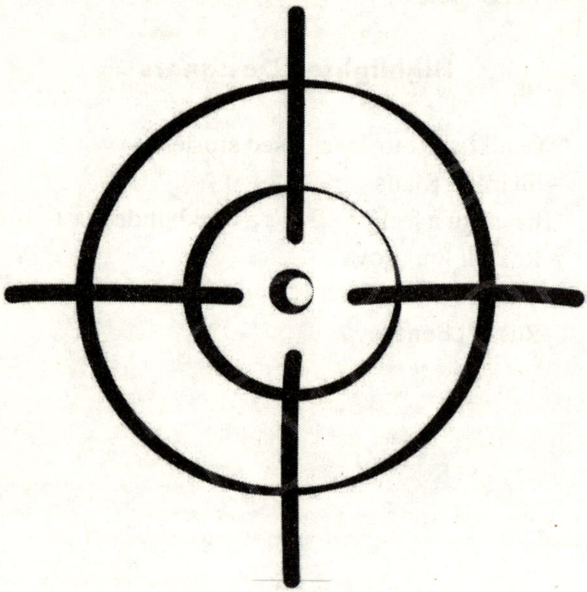

STEP 2: ESTABLISH YOUR PRINCIPLES

> *"And so I think that has been kind of an interesting obstacle to overcome—trusting in myself to be able to do this and do it on our own. And trusting that, yes, we had something that was worth pursuing."*
>
> **—Fran Dunaway, cofounder and CEO, TomboyX**

WHAT ARE PRINCIPLES?

The principles and beliefs that we have today were embedded in us when we were kids. They represent the code that we set for ourselves, through which everything we evaluate gets filtered. Everyone has principles, but I bet if you asked people to share theirs with you, they wouldn't know what to say.

Your principles are uniquely yours. They allow you to move throughout the world based on a compass that you define. They don't have to be "Ten Commandments" lofty, because there are already societal principles that most of us generally subscribe to (such as not killing people and not cheating on your spouse). The principles we are talking about here are the ones that drive your everyday conduct, whether in your business or personal relationships. They are designed to help you avoid getting whiplash when a situation arises and you aren't sure what to do. You might ask yourself, "How do my principles apply here?"

The most well-known architect of principles is Ray Dalio, the famous hedge fund manager who wrote a book conveniently titled *Principles*. In it, Dalio codified how he would act differently in the future based on mistakes he had made in the past. By embedding those principles deeply into the fabric of his organization, he created a set of rules and behaviors that significantly reduced drama and optimized decision-making.

There is tremendous value to embedding principles inside of your organization, even if the approach is a fraction of Dalio's sophistication. But the more fundamental value comes when you embed principles in your life first. Without principles for how you run "You, Inc.," it will be difficult to lead an organization based on the same premise.

I created some principles for myself a couple of years ago. Just the act of writing down how I wanted to live my life was so powerful. I felt a bit of shame that I was only then writing down this code. What the hell had I been doing for the past forty years? It was like I was waking up every day and letting the winds of circumstance dictate my life, just reacting on the fly. No compass. But principles provide a shield. Each principle becomes this little container that defines your behavior, and within that container, there are ways that behavior manifests itself. Now, whenever the chaos swirls around you, you can look to your principles as your guide. Here are mine.

Principles

I approach my life with a daily intention to pursue fun and adventure.
We get to choose how we interact with people and situations and can choose for it to be stressful or a source of energy and enjoyment.

I keep my financial overhead in check to give my family and myself flexibility to have experiences without being overly stressed about money.

Adventure also means that I have invested well enough in my health to be able to do the things that I want to do.

I care deeply about understanding the needs and wants of people around me.
I'm interested in understanding the shoes that other people walk in and make sure I'm clear on that before I share my position.

I show gratitude in small ways often.
I get a lot of satisfaction from doing things like:

- *Helping make someone's day by buying a friend (or even a total stranger) a cup of coffee at Starbucks.*
- *Acknowledging small victories.*
- *Introducing people where I think there is mutual benefit.*
- *Checking in on people to see how they are doing.*
- *When someone shines a light on my blind spot, I get curious and appreciate it.*
- *When someone is up for acknowledgment or an award, I celebrate their accomplishment.*

I do not gossip.

Talking about other people in a way that is not constructive to a goal or outcome is a waste of energy with no positive result.

I speak up when my feelings are in conflict with my thoughts and actions.

I am not afraid to let people know when a situation arises that risks compromising my principles.

If I am feeling unable to unlock my feelings, I do not hesitate to find someone who can help me.

I approach conflict with a sense of curiosity, not aggression or defensiveness.

I think about my time with intention.

That doesn't mean I don't relax or chill out, but I do it with intention, so that my time blocks are well managed. I like making sure that my time (work and play) is intentional.

I do business with people that I like and trust, regardless of the outcome.

I realize that we can't control the outcomes, but I do want to enjoy the journey. The "No assholes" rule is in force!

When there is music that moves me, I dance without apology.

I'm OK dancing to the beat of my own drum and not worrying about what other people are doing. If it's a speech or a dance or a poem or whatever, if it gives me energy, I do it.

I am on time.

I make a point to be on time because it aligns with integrity and honoring commitments.

I value when other people are on time.

A few thoughts on these principles. First, principles are not values. Values tend to be more vague (think of concepts like teamwork) and name a category but not behavior. Principles, on the other hand, are behaviors that are clear and measurable. Second, principles are living and can be updated and clarified for new circumstances. Over time, I have added sub-bullets to show how principles might be applied to make them more tangible so they are relevant to my life. Third, I have to acknowledge the risk that if these principles aren't embedded or coded into my life, I likely won't remember or recall them in the moment when they're most needed.

Dalio talks a lot about coding principles into business and the sophisticated way this plays out at his hedge fund, Bridgewater. Let's take that concept and think about how our principles can be automated in our own life design. For example, I have coded the principle of showing gratitude in small ways. I often purchase twenty $5 Starbucks gift cards at a time and keep them with me in my bag, where they're easily accessible. For the principle of being on time, I have an assistant who confirms every appointment with the people I'm meeting, increasing the likelihood that the individual will be on time themselves. Not everything can be so easily codified, but the effort is well worth it to make the most impact in your design.

WHY PRINCIPLES ARE PART OF LIFE DESIGN

Principles are fundamental to life design. Without them, there is too much variability, and it is difficult to see patterns and learn from them. Here are the primary reasons principles are so foundational:

Principles Allow People to Know You

Having principles makes it easier to share yourself with others. When conflict emerges, it is amazing how many stories get created about what the other person might be thinking. With principles, it is easier for people to understand you. Try this comment, or your own variation of it, the next time conflict emerges for you.

> *"I want you to know me and see how I think about this situation. The reason I am acting or reacting the way that I am is that I have a principle around XYZ, and this is how it applies in this situation. I'm not saying it's right or wrong, but hopefully it helps you get to know me a bit better."*

It Is Hard for People to Attack Your Principles

If you are in a situation where you are feeling uneasy about the direction that a conversation is going but you haven't expressed yourself, you might say something like "I have a principle to share when what I am feeling is in conflict with what I'm thinking and saying. Therefore, I'd like to clear that up."

What makes that so powerful is that it is difficult for people to attack principles. Principles are yours to own. They are your rocks. You are just living in accordance with them, and that's integrity. How people react to you is not your responsibility. Your responsibility is to act in accordance with what you have said is your guidebook for the life you live.

"Living my principles is not about making everyone happy."
–Fran Dunaway, cofounder and CEO, TomboyX

I was a partner in a media strategies firm, and I'd been working with this guy for about fifteen years. I had started out as a seasonal worker and then became an employee and then became a partner. And we were very close friends and had known each other a long time, and I had kind of helped his career by producing and executive-producing and bringing a sense of filmmaking to the political ad world.

But when I started what became TomboyX on the side, I said, "Look, this will be as much time as you spend with your family and on the golf course, and it's just my side project that I'm going to be doing." Because I truly thought it was just going to make some shirts. And he became like a jealous lover. It was something that he wasn't really excited about, and he tried to undermine it in a lot of different ways and pooh-pooh it. I know he was afraid or didn't want me to go away or any of this stuff. So, I mean I knew that that was part of it, but it just kept getting incrementally more and more uncomfortable.

And I remember he called me on a Sunday. I picked up the phone and the first words out of his mouth were

"I'm going to talk and you're going to listen." And in that moment, it just clicked. I knew I was done. I didn't have a safety net. I needed insurance. I needed all these things. But then I talked, and an hour later, I think he heard me because I ended the conversation with "I'm done. D-O-N-E done." And I hung up the phone.

And it was like doors opening of recognition of how throughout the years I've been undermined or dismissed or not as valued. And I honestly think it was because of my gender. And he somehow felt his stardom would be diminished if he were to give me equal credit. And so, he liked me being in the background but didn't want me being up in the front. So, he just kind of kept me in my place, and I went along with it for the longest time.

Until I didn't.

You Will Make Decisions More Clearly

When you are grounded in your principles, it is a lot easier to make decisions and communicate those decisions in a way that people will understand. Principles are an effective way to eliminate the noise of a particular situation. Principles take the emotional edge off. You do what you do because you are guided by a set of principles for how you organize decision-making in your life. There is nothing to apologize for. It is who you are.

Casey Roloff founded Seabrook based on a set of principles. Everything he does is driven by how he believes communities should be built, such as maximizing connection to each other and the environment, in a movement called New Urbanism. While he has built an incredible community, what is most impressive is that he has built a mental framework about what aligns and does not align with his vision. With all of Casey's success, you can imagine how many people come to him with ways that he can make more money. Because of his principles, Casey can respond not just to the moment or the situation but based on what he knows he wants to create.

"Town-building is a higher form of art."
–Casey Roloff, founder and CEO, Seabrook

At Seabrook, we make decisions based on the principle that town-building is like art. Most of the industry thinks about it as what's inside the home and the lot. But it doesn't harmonize with the rest of the community. So when you take an urban planning approach, it's more about what is outside of the building. We work on how to organize buildings in a way that creates an incredible experience for the pedestrian.

I kind of describe it like a chef, where the difference between a good chef and a great chef is that a great chef knows not only how to make amazing food but also how to put it together with other foods that complement each other, and then they know how to create a beautiful package on a plate where you're just like, "Oh my gosh, I don't even want to eat it. It's so beautiful." But then you eat it, and it's even more amazing, right? And then you can take the quality of the table and just keep going further and further out. You go to the entrance and outside the building and to the parking lot and the street.

For us, town-building is the highest form of art. It doesn't start with artists selling art in galleries. Everything will look better and taste better when the planning of the environment is right.

You Will Build a Solid Foundation

My business partner, Eric Page, often likes to ask, "What principle are we employing here?" I appreciate that question, because it forces me to pause before reacting to a particular circumstance or situation. Principles are foundational. Everything that gets built on top of them (your personal relationships, your professional career, your commitment to health, etc.) is stacked atop the groundwork that you have laid.

If your principles are frequently compromised or you haven't yet established them clearly, then you might find yourself more anxious than you would like. Why? Well, without a strong foundation of principles, structures are vulnerable to small changes in the environment, and it doesn't take much for those vulnerabilities to get exposed. When money is at stake or a deal is in the works, hang on to your seat. These are the times when the structure gets shaky. Sarah Dusek felt it when she was raising money for Under Canvas. But because of her strong foundational principles, she maintained her commitment to not just taking the money and "figuring it out later."

"Beware money masked as power."
–Sarah Dusek, cofounder and former CEO, Under Canvas

It was one of those really heart-wrenching scenarios. We had bootstrapped our business through our own sweat and tears with our own cash, which was virtually nonexistent, and were trying to do more than we had the capital to do. I had knocked on probably a million venture capital doors and heard the common refrain "You're not a tech company." I wasn't well connected, so when we finally got a term sheet from a high-profile firm I was excited. But the term sheet, despite our best efforts to negotiate, was very one-sided. It gave so much power and so many rights to the investors, even though they were buying a minority stake.

When I questioned the term sheet and tried to negotiate, the response I received was "If you don't take this term sheet, you won't be getting money from anyone, because this is the deal that venture capitalists do. We have the money, and therefore we have the power." At which point, I thought to myself, *If I had any doubts about doing this deal before, I certainly cannot do this deal now. I believe that money doesn't have to mean total power, and I don't think that that means you have to treat the little person with disrespect.*

I realized at that moment that I can't get into bed with someone who doesn't think I am their equal partner. I realized I'm constantly going to be at odds with this person and this fund, because I so intrinsically believe in fairness and equality. That moment helped me crystallize what I really valued. It was like it slapped me in the face and said, *This is what I believe.* And you know, sometimes we don't know what we believe until our views are challenged in some way. I turned down that deal with my business in horrific jeopardy, and it forced us to go back to the drawing board and ask, "What are we going to do now?" because I can't do business like this. It ended up solidifying our values, though, and we ultimately found more capital ($20 million), and we found partners who had our values and who saw things the same way we did. They were transparent about what they wanted, and we could work with that. I waited for the right money, the right partners, and the right structure, and this was pivotal to changing the course of the company that we built.

WHEN YOU COMPROMISE YOUR PRINCIPLES, THINGS GO SIDEWAYS

Compromising your principles is called being out of integrity. When how you feel and what you think are different from what you communicate, you are misaligned. It happens all the time. We don't want to hurt people's feelings. We want to get something by withholding our true beliefs. Or we think it can wait until after we meet our near-term goal. But the truth is that whenever I have tried to sweep things under the rug or kick the can down the road, it always comes back to bite me in the ass, 100 percent of the time. Here are a couple of examples:

The Risk of Compromising Principles

In 2013, I had the opportunity to sign a big contract with a health insurer to provide our software to their members. We had created a "mileage rewards program for health," a way for individuals to track their fitness and earn rewards from their health plan. The contract offered meaningful (and necessary) cash for our business, but I knew that it had a lot of potential for problems.

First, there were no guarantees that they would roll it out within a given time period, which meant that I wouldn't learn that quickly what worked and what didn't. Second, the nature of the relationship relegated us to building a lot of custom features for the client when we were, in fact, trying to sell our software to many different clients. Third, the person that would be responsible for overseeing our account managed through fear-based tactics.

So guess what I did. I signed the deal, rationalizing that I would be able to resolve the open issues over time. In short, I compromised my principles. I was scared that if we didn't sign this deal, everything would go to shit, and we wouldn't be able to build a business. And do you know what happened? I spent the next two years in pain, trying to crawl out from that compromise. We didn't get exposed to sufficient consumers to learn how to improve the product. We built a lot of custom functionality, and most of it never got used. And I subjected myself to getting bullied by an insurance company vice president.

In short, I knew it was a bad deal going in, but I didn't live my principles—and the results were predictable.

Now, it's easy to look at this and say, *Hey, you did what you had to do under the circumstances. You needed the capital to grow your business. Anybody would have done the same thing.* Maybe, but the point is that I chipped away at my integrity and represented something different from what I was feeling. In doing so, I participated in a dynamic that fueled further resentment and frustration.

Would a better outcome have resulted had I not compromised? That is a tricky question. It is possible that being up front would have produced a better result. It is also possible that we would not have completed the transaction, and I would have saved myself a couple of years of struggle. It really gets to how you define the outcome. I have yet to have an experience where I compromised my principles and it all worked out in the end. In the end, in fact, compromising my principles has never worked out. In the long term, being out of integrity creates layers of armor that protect you from being exposed. And eventually, layer after layer, you forget your principles and live behind walls of compromise, afraid to reveal your authentic self.

Exercise: Creating Your Principles

There are many books and articles about living up to your principles, but it's essential to establish your baseline principles. If someone asked you to list your principles, what would you say? Seems pretty simple, but it's not obvious to most of us. How do you figure out what your principles are?

Below is a process that will help you develop and document principles for your life design. Keep in mind that you don't want to have so many principles you forget what they are. My suggestion is to max out at ten.

Step 1: Build a Mind Map. I use tools like Miro (www.miro.com) to create a mind map to brainstorm principles. Think about times in your life where you compromised yourself (for instance, with friends, work, or relationships) and how a clear set of principles might have helped guide you.

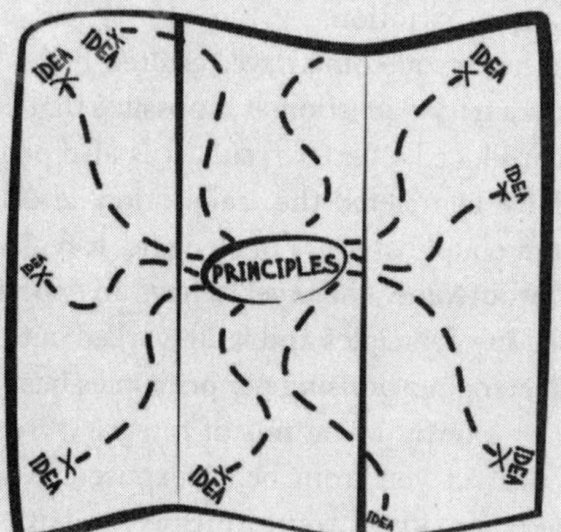

Step 2: Prioritize. Take the brainstormed items and insert them into a worksheet. Create two columns, one for frequency and the other for intensity. For frequency, rate how often you estimate that principle getting used (high, medium, or low frequency). For intensity, rate how intense it would be for you to either sacrifice that standard or adhere to it (high, medium, or low intensity). Prioritize your list based on letting the higher frequency and higher intensity principles rise up.

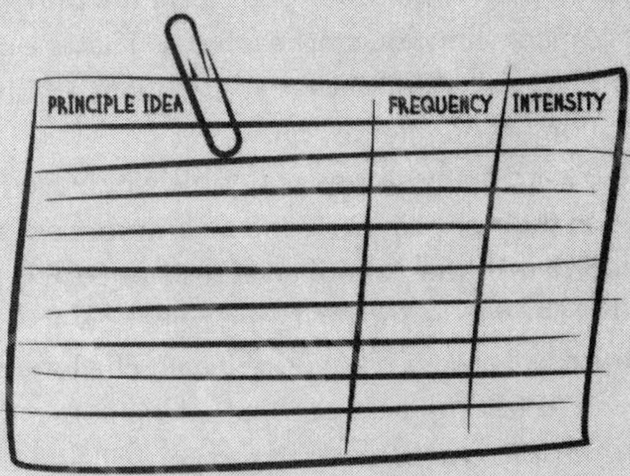

Step 3: Define Your Principles. Now, what does each principle mean to you? Create a clear definition and include specific examples. Clarity of thought is important here. Don't skimp on this step.

Step 4: Make Them Visible and Embed Them. Write down your top principles (no more than ten) and their definitions in a format you can easily reference. Then, next to each principle, write down one way that you can embed it so that it doesn't require you to remember it.

Step 5: Learn and Iterate. As you move through the next month, choose one principle to focus on and put into practice. Don't try to tackle them all at once! What situations arose where you applied the principle? How did it resolve? How were you able to recall it more easily throughout the month? Make modifications and iterate as the principles you want to live by crystallize for you.

PRO TIP: Print these out, laminate them, and stick them on a wall in your bathroom. Give the principles a quick glance when you start each day. That is a great way to orient your daily living in accordance with the foundation of your life design.

There are many stories of people who have grappled with their principles, faced a compromise, and decided to take the path of least resistance. It is the path that seems the most alluring right now—but the long term will always create significant challenges. Get used to flexing the muscle of asking yourself, *What principle is at play here?* and you will feel significantly lighter as you move through life. It is a life design hack that will save you from a lot of distress.

ESTABLISH YOUR PRINCIPLES
CHAPTER SUMMARY

Principles are one of the most overlooked, but most important, pillars of life design. Without them, we spend a lot of time flapping in the wind, vulnerable to the wishes of others. When principles work in coordination with your ability to separate stories from facts, your foundation will be solid. Here are the key highlights from this chapter.

- Principles are yours to own. They represent the code that you use to filter the decisions you make in your life, big and small.
- Principles are not values. Principles are behaviors.
- Principles are foundational, are difficult to attack, and will help you see situations more clearly.
- When you compromise your principles, you know it—you feel it. It is called being out of integrity.
- Don't leave your principles to chance. Create them and make them visible. Embed them in your life so you can better access them in your day to day.

ESTABLISH YOUR PRINCIPLES
CHAPTER SUMMARY

The Exercise in This Chapter

- Creating Your Principles

Highlighted Designers

- "Living my principles is not about making everyone happy."
  —Fran Dunaway
- "Town-building is a higher form of art."
  —Casey Roloff
- "Beware money masked as power."
  —Sarah Dusek
- The Risk of Compromising Principles

STEP 3: HARNESS ENERGY FROM THE ENVIRONMENT

"I made the choice to get clean and to start over. And I tried everything, and the only thing that ever stuck for me was reaching out to a source greater than myself. I call it the universe or drawing on energy that helps me be my best self. And that kind of catapulted me into this spiritual journey where everything is exactly how it's supposed to be."

—Max Nelson, founder and CEO, HOOD

WHAT IS ENERGY, AND WHERE DOES IT COME FROM?

Trail running has become an integral part of my life. Every weekend, you will find me in the mountains before daybreak, with nothing but a headlamp, water, bars, gel nutrition, the trail, and my mind. It is simple. It is free of distractions. It is a face-to-face encounter with humility. It is the place where I am reminded that life requires endurance. It is where I can appreciate being healthy. It's also where I can hang out with some friends and talk about stupid things that are funny and meaningless, like what is going to happen with Bitcoin or why I should use wet wipes versus toilet paper when I go to the bathroom or how many toenails I lost on that last ultra race. I know, silly. But the trails are an important source of energy for my life.

We all draw energy from somewhere. How do I know? Because the fact is that energy governs the laws of the universe and gives us the ability to do work. In life design, your source of energy and how you use it matters because it directly influences your ability to perform at your best and be your best.

There is a certain energy, a strength, that I feel when I am doing exactly what I want to be doing, doing it where I want to be doing it, and doing it with whom I want to be doing it with. I feel lighter, happier, better able to absorb challenges. I know you know that feeling. Close your eyes and tap into that for a moment.

I learned about the concept of energy in my life from Lex Sisney, my friend and coach and the author of *Organizational Physics*. He helped me appreciate that life design is a function of **(i) how I maximize the energy that I have, (ii) how I reduce the drains on my energy, and (iii) how I source new energy.** Don't worry, this isn't a science book—but consider that science can explain how we can better design our lives. Let's look at the first two laws of thermodynamics, shall we?

The first law of thermodynamics states that energy cannot be created or destroyed. It is a constant that can only be redistributed or changed from one form to another.

The second law of thermodynamics states that over time, systems fall apart due to entropy, or disorder.

OK, science class is over! Now let's understand why energy is such a profound principle of life design.

The idea that our energy is a constant as expressed in the first law means that to get more energy, we have to source it from somewhere, and that somewhere is what we call the environment. Once we have energy, the second law states that it will begin to dissipate. Available energy will first combat the entropy, or disorder, in the system so that the structure stays up. What remains can be used for continued growth. Maximize energy. Reduce entropy. That's physics.

TAP INTO THE ENVIRONMENT

A critical ingredient of life design is drawing energy from the people and places around you (i.e., your environment) to help you do your work. It is about drawing in energy that inspires creativity, freedom, curiosity, and possibility.

Think about your life and the places and people that give you energy. Where have you felt the most alive? What is it about a particular location, activity, or group of people that makes you feel inspired, creative, and free?

I didn't realize the profound impact that my physical environment had on me until my family and I moved to Costa Rica in 2018. The drive to change our environment was that I felt lost. I felt like my career was blocked. My relationship with my wife was blocked. I needed to break out of my trajectory, but I was scared. I knew that everything I was feeling and believing was just something I was making up in my head, but I couldn't shake it. I didn't have the skills to acknowledge my fears or the language to articulate them. All I knew was that I felt suffocated, and the life trajectory I was on was massively draining my energy.

The intention to "flip our script" and move abroad was grounded in a decision that my wife and I made to commit to a life partnership, to build a foundation that would protect and honor our commitment to each other. We made the decision to make a life change not because we wanted to run away from something but because we wanted to run toward a new opportunity and a new frontier. We wanted to put our life on a new trajectory. We wanted more energy.

The Drive to Change Our Environment

Melissa and I had spent some time with Phil, our business coach, getting reconnected and using some new tools to interact with one another in a way that was a lot less about blame and more about owning our own experience. It was bringing us closer together, and we started to enjoy the idea of plotting out a future as partners where we built a fence around the power of our relationship versus individual fences around ourselves. On a check-in with our coach, Melissa mentioned the idea that we had fantasized about for many years, spending a year abroad as a family.

"Hmmm," Phil said. "Where would you go?"

"We don't know," we answered. "But we get a lot of energy talking about it."

"Why don't you do it after the kids get out of school this year?" Phil asked.

"Oh, we couldn't do that. The timing isn't right," I said.

"Isn't it?" said Phil. "You're working for a company where your year commitment will end there. You have a son still in middle school and a son going into sixth grade. Isn't it an optimal time to do it?"

Time seemed to slow down, *Matrix* style, as my gaze met Melissa's. We didn't know what to say, so we said, "Maybe you're right. Hmmm. Let's think about it."

The match was lit.

Adding Fuel to the Possibility

Over the course of the next couple of weeks, we kept talking about realizing this opportunity. I could feel a deep excitement starting to well up inside me. By coincidence, sitting on our coffee table was the November 2017 issue of *National Geographic*, highlighting the happiest places on Earth. On the cover? Costa Rica. That sounded kind of awesome. Why not? We each spoke a little bit of Spanish and loved the idea of researching it.

The flame started to grow.

I reached out to my Entrepreneurs' Organization (EO) network in Costa Rica. A previous neighbor's father lived there, as did several business school alumni. I got on the phone. I got excited. People started introducing me to others. My confidence built. *Holy shit, I think we could do this.*

The flame was now a straight-up fire.

And here is the key: for the first time in a long time, Melissa and I were doing this together, despite the uncertainty and the perceived risk.

Melissa's primary feeling in our relationship was a lack of safety, but she was jumping into something that seemingly had some risks: big expense, new language, no real connections, kids' school, living situation, jobs. I can't think of a more unsafe thing to do than up and move to another country. But we were doing it, and we were excited about it.

My primary feeling in our relationship was judgment, but Melissa was supporting my enthusiasm. I was getting a ton of energy because this felt like a start-up, with lots of uncertainty, a vision, energy, and a commitment to create something new.

I felt excited and alive and inspired. We weren't doing this for anyone else. We were doing this because Melissa and I had chosen to build a fence around our relationship, and this was our construction site. I wasn't trying to one-up anyone or prove that I was successful. I was just going to live my life, and this was what we wanted to do. This was giving us energy. So we leapt toward freedom.

By the end of December, we were clear. It was going to happen.

Our decision to move to Costa Rica was one of the boldest moves we have made as a family. There was no more talking about it or fantasizing about the possibility. It was happening. And that clarity, that unambiguous articulation of intent, not only gave our energy a clear path, but we attracted energy from people who could help us on our journey. Not only that, but when we finally settled in Costa Rica, we felt the power of welcoming new energy into our life from the environment and people we met, and the virtuous flywheel began to move with little effort. We felt lucky.

HOW TO MAXIMIZE THE ENERGY YOU HAVE

Here are three ways to maximize the energy in your life right now:

Maintain the Right Mind-Set

It is a stretch to think that we are always going to be in an environment where we gain energy. That's not realistic. But you don't need to be in Costa Rica to harness the energy, even though Costa Rica is amazing. You don't need to be in that yoga class or doing meditation. You don't need to be with a specific person to harness the energy that is inside of you. What you want is to access those feelings of being in those moments and work to make them your standard for how you show up in the world.

> Can I be in that Costa Rica mind-set even if I'm living in Seattle?

> Can I feel appreciation for this person, even though I am growing impatient?

> Can I feel the warmth of my friendships, wherever I am?
>
> Can I stay aligned with my principles, regardless of the circumstance?

Getting unstuck is the ability to recall the positive feelings of a past experience, because that is what will remain long after the moment. It is one reason that meditation and journaling are effective techniques that can help you hold on to that energy and wire your brain to more consistently maintain a high-energy state of mind.

Give More Than You Get

Energy is not just for consumption. It is also about creation. Giving energy to others turns you into a tractor beam that draws people into your orbit. And the more energy you give, the more you will get. We know those people with a magnetism that makes us feel great when we are around them. What is it about them? How do they seem to navigate through life unencumbered, where you're thinking, *How do I get some of that?* You can be that person.

Casey Roloff is definitely that guy. Everyone loves Casey, and for good reason. He genuinely cares for people around him and creates experiences that make them feel comfortable. For Casey, life is about giving people energy. He has built a town, intentionally designed for people to feel welcomed and connected. He sheepishly calls it the "disease to please." I call it a gift and his genius zone!

The Disease to Please

–Casey Roloff, founder, Seabrook

A lot of what shapes us is our childhood, right? I had a very uncomfortable, awkward school experience. When it came to school, I wasn't studious and just felt like a nobody, and I hated when people made me uncomfortable. And so from those experiences of being bullied, I have always wanted to create something that was super-inclusive, where everyone felt welcomed, and everyone felt appreciated.

It's easier to say, harder to do, but I don't want anyone to ever feel dumb. It could be in a meeting, or with a housekeeper or a maintenance person. I want everyone to feel important and never be judged by how they look or, you know, any of those things. To some extent I call it the disease to please. I think I heard that on *Oprah*. I just want everyone to feel welcomed and loved and appreciated. And it's just a weird obsession.

Have Clear Intention

When you are clear on the life that you are designing, it's a lot easier to maximize your energy. Said from the opposite angle, when you're stuck, your energy gets mismanaged because it doesn't know where to go.

Don't put off life design work and wait until you have things "figured out" or are in a "better place." When you defer your life design until everything is in place, you miss the entire purpose of how effective energy can be for you right now. Consider these energy-wasting statements:

> *"I'm not where I want to be, but when I get there, things will be great."*
>
> *"I can slog it out for now and see what happens."*
>
> *"I'm not in a good spot, but let me just power through it. It will get better."*

Try letting go of needing to have it all figured out. Try letting go of an outcome. As I like to say, "Let the universe do its work." Try these maximizing, energy-giving intentions:

> *"I have everything I need right now."*
>
> *"I am in control, and I don't rely on hope to design my life."*
>
> *"I make mistakes, but I am always learning, always improving."*

Once you do that, you get to be open and ready when a great opportunity presents itself, just like it did for Max Nelson.

"If it's good enough for Jay-Z, well. . . ."
—Max Nelson, founder and CEO, HOOD

Let me tell you a story about the universe conspiring to support my vision. It's September 2018, and I'm scrolling through Instagram one night. I'm getting ready to go to bed and stumble across a photo of Jay-Z wearing our Bel-Air hat. My heart starts racing. How is this possible? So, this is nuts. This is the moment I was waiting for, because I was so convinced that he was the right type of guy to represent this fashion.

I go through my Shopify and track down every single Bel-Air order we've ever fulfilled. And I Google everybody who's purchased the hats, and it was his private chef. I tracked him down. It was a gift. His private chef bought the hat. That hat was paid for off our website and gifted to him. It gets better. You're going to freak when I tell you this.

We got a fan. Jay-Z's a fan. So, I started looking for inspiration. I said, OK, he's wearing the Bel-Air hat, he lives in Bel-Air. Where's he from? He's from Brooklyn, Marcy Projects, Brooklyn. Let me make a Marcy hat. OK, what else? I started listening to his music. 560 State Street. He talks about that in his song. And that's the address of the building where he lived in Fort Greene when he was a drug dealer. Let me make a 560 State Street hat. I'm making these hats with no clear way of knowing how I'm going to get them to him. But I know that the universe will conspire, because it already has. It's already destined to happen.

So, I just do the work and I make the hats and I sit on the hats for three months. I don't do anything with them. They're just sitting there. OK? And it's a Tuesday morning now, in 2019. I call my friend Kabir, and he's a banker and we're just rapping. And I said, "What are you up to?" And he goes, "I'm actually heading to Rock Nation right now. I'm meeting with the CEO, Jay Brown, who's a friend of mine." I go, "Oh my God, that's crazy. Yeah. You know, I made the hat that Jay-Z was wearing. And I made two other hats. I made a Marcy and a State Street hat." My friend says, "Send me the pictures now, and I'll show them to Jay Brown when I'm done meeting with him."

And he has a meeting with Jay Brown. He shows him the pictures, and Jay Brown says, "Send me the hats, and I'll get them to Jay-Z." I send the hats over to Jay Brown and within seventy-two hours, Jay-Z is seen photographed at an art opening wearing the Marcy hat and then forty-eight hours after that, he's photographed wearing the State Street hat with Beyoncé, and then both of them get posted.

So, then it gets even better. The Sunday before the pandemic and everything gets shut down, I'm at Staples Center at the Lakers-Clippers game, and I see Jay Brown, CEO of Rock Nation. I've never met him in person. I don't want to go up to him and interrupt. I said to my girlfriend, "You know what, if I'm supposed to talk to him today, we're going to run into each other. Don't be that guy that's hanging over him on his court seats when he's with his kid."

So the game ends and we're leaving Staples Center. There are hundreds of people out there. I turn around one last time before we head to the car, and I see Jay Brown walking by. I have to talk to him. "Jay," I said. "It's Max Nelson, from HOOD." And he looks at me and says, "Buddy, good job, man. Good job. Keep it up. Keep it up. Keep getting me those hats. It's a great product. Jay-Z loves it. I love it. We love it. And it's good to meet you."

And it's like moments like that, that have kind of defined the two-year journey. You know, the universe just saying, *Keep going, keep going. You got this.*

HOW TO REDUCE YOUR ENERGY DRAINS

You are likely expending too much of your available energy fighting entropy, so your energy drains.

Think about having a hundred available points of energy per day. If you spend fifty points on entropy, that gives you fifty remaining points toward intention. That ratio is 1:1. If you only needed twenty-five points for entropy, that would leave seventy-five points for intention, a ratio of 3:1 in favor of your intentions. Small changes in how you use your energy can create big rewards. Get unstuck by significantly reducing the entropy in your life so you have more space available to harness what gives you energy to thrive.

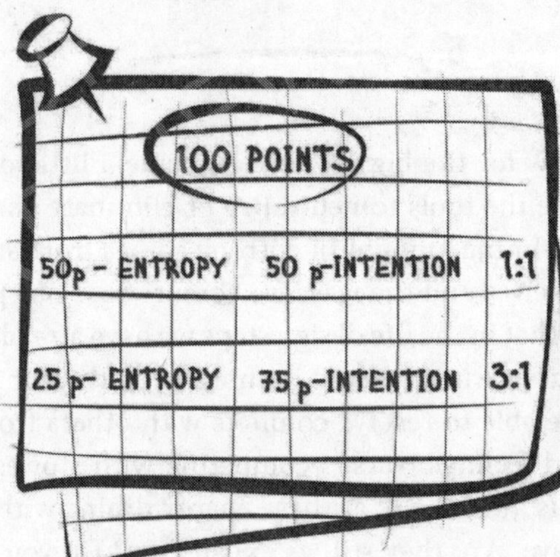

If you don't neutralize the entropy, the energy drains in your life, and you won't have room to welcome new energy for the intentional work ahead. It is also easier to identify what drains our energy before expressing all the things that will give us more energy. That's because we feel it inside of us even though we may not want to acknowledge it.

But we can write it down. We can identify it. Entropy could be stress at work, strained relationships, or anything else that is dragging you down. It could also be your own self-talk about your physical or mental health. Do it now. Think about five things in your life that drain your energy. Be honest with yourself. It doesn't have to be about other people. It is courageous to write these down.

1. ______________________
2. ______________________
3. ______________________
4. ______________________
5. ______________________

And now for the big secret. Yes, come a little closer. You already have the tools to neutralize or eliminate entropy. Yes! An overwhelming amount of entropy comes from stories that we tell ourselves and the ways we compromise our principles. You nailed that in the life design steps we have already covered. Think about it: when you are in integrity with your principles and you are able to resolve conflicts with others from a place of facts and feelings (versus competing with stories), a lot of entropy falls away. Look at these energy drains with the tools that you have. Are they still as exhausting? Do you feel more equipped to address them?

Getting unstuck is about reducing entropy, and with entropy reduced, it is now time to welcome new energy into your life and begin to get on top of actualizing your life design.

HOW TO WELCOME NEW ENERGY INTO YOUR LIFE

1. Focus on inputs.
2. Let go of your shame.
3. Seek approval from within.
4. Whatever happens is perfect.
5. Be bold.

Making the move to Costa Rica at what originally seemed like the least opportune time for our kids and careers was the best thing that ever happened to us. I say this because the decision was grounded in true, authentic intention. We were not doing this for anyone else. We had no expectations on the outcome. Whatever happened would unfold as it would unfold. It was the first time I was really doing something to prioritize my family that wasn't tied to my career. And still I wondered, *What will people think? What am I going to do? What will my life look like? Will I be relevant?* All these stories and all these fears surfaced about my identity, my failures, and my shame. There was no hiding. We were moving to Central America.

And then great things just started to happen. I let go of needing to be in control. I was open to the possibility of new people, new experiences, and new energy. My intention was presence, patience, and possibility.

So when my former business partner, Eric, reached out to me to invite me to get involved with a new business venture, I was open and curious. I was ready. And I had no idea where it would take me. I embraced the new energy. Today I am the cofounder of an outsourced bookkeeping and accounting firm called Stride Services. We serve business owners by providing them with the back-office support that can keep them focused on achieving their highest and best staying in their genius zone.

Would I have ended up owning an accounting business if I had stayed in Seattle? Probably not. My identity was so wrapped up in the expectations and approval of others that the idea of getting into a service business as "unsexy" as bookkeeping and accounting would never have crossed my mind. The very act of sourcing new energy in my life gave me the positive headspace to reconcile the blocks that had held me back.

Now it's your turn to welcome new energy into your life. Here is how.

Focus on Inputs

Get out of the mind-set that there "should" be a specific outcome. When you constrain energy to a specific outcome, you lose out on all the other possibilities. For all of you who associate success with controlling a result, this one is a mindbender for sure. Your possibilities can't grow if you can't let go. They grow when the potential positive outcomes are numerous.

Controlling Values, Not Timelines

Alissa Leinonen is the founder and CEO of Gourmondo, a regional catering firm in Seattle, Washington. I'm not sure that the Alissa of eighteen years ago, running a little store by Pike Place Market, ever imagined that she would employ over three hundred people and operate cafés inside some of the world's major tech companies.

What is so incredible about Alissa is that it's never been about the business. It has always been about amazing food and empowering her team to be the very best that they can be. She is the mother hen of the company, and while she has architected a business that allows her to work only two days per week (yes, totally jealous), she is also the first one to give holiday gifts to the families, host company-wide parties with family members, and support minimum wage employees when they need financial aid. Gourmondo is simply a vehicle to deliver happiness, and she does so in spades. When Ernst & Young recognized Alissa as an Entrepreneur of the Year, it signaled that Alissa had definitely found her groove.

Let Go of Shame

Shame is a real snake, and it is often connected to the people and circumstances that are in close physical proximity. The lens through which you evaluate yourself is highly influenced by how you think others evaluate you. *Am I enough? Why did I make that decision? Look at how I screwed that situation up!*

So much of our worth tends to be measured by others (peers, parents, colleagues, customers, partners), and shame is pervasive. You can't run away from shame, but you can reduce its impact by creating a new environment that fills you up and gives you energy to create and think and act. What other people think about you is none of your business. A key strategy for shifting away from shame is to ground your stories with facts and grab the belief bubbles that give you energy.

I had to let go of some shame and liberate myself to be the type of person I wanted to be, regardless of what other people think about me. Only then could I contemplate starting a new business venture that was for me and not for anyone else.

Seek Approval from Within

As my coach Phil used to say, "Live your worth. Don't prove your worth." What he meant was that I have nothing to prove to anyone else—and neither do you. You are *already* worthy. You are not your work or your business. The very fact that you are here and investing in yourself and living in accordance with your principles is all that matters.

One of the best ways to know if you are an approval seeker is that you feel great when people acknowledge your accomplishments, and a bit empty when you aren't getting outside feedback. If you're reliant on others' approval, you'll set out for another milestone to get that hit of approval after every accomplishment and just stay on that hamster wheel.

We all appreciate external validation, of course. However, if it is the basis for how you perceive your value, you will always be disappointed. Why? Because we don't control how others view us, and frankly, who is to say that the approval we are getting is from someone whose principles we admire and want to emulate? You may not even like that person very much but want their approval because they have power, or they are your boss or a potential new client. You may find yourself violating your own principles to get their positive feedback and constantly feeling out of integrity.

Think back to a time when you sought approval from someone who you really didn't care for and compromised your principles to get it. How did it go? How did you feel? How much energy did you lose in trying to recover from that compromise?

"Nobody cares as much about me as I think they do."
—Kirby Winfield, general partner, Ascend VC

I wasn't done yet. I hadn't achieved the huge outcome that I wanted. I had some good results, but I still had something to prove. And I was angry because I was needed at home, but I felt the need to go after the shiny ring. My daughter had been born with special needs. My wife was at home. And I was out in Vegas for my buddy's bachelor party, the exact opposite of where I needed to be. When I reflect on that time, I see that I was certainly driven by fear—fear of not being loved or fear of not being admired.

I have always been externally driven. I wanted people to like me, to laugh at my jokes. I have always been very aware of social dynamics and power imbalances from an early age, and my wife tells me how exhausting it must be for me to constantly be creating these hierarchies in my head. And it is. And even when I got the big results, it was never fulfilling, so why did it matter what others thought? Nobody really cares as much about me as I think they do. They have their own lives. And I looked at myself in 2013, and I was unhealthy and overweight and prediabetic, and I stopped chasing other people's expectations for a minute. I finally stopped and asked myself the question of whether I really enjoyed what I was doing.

Since then, I have lost fifty pounds. I run six miles a day. And I started an investment firm called Ascend VC to help seed other aspiring entrepreneurs to achieve their dreams.

Note: As I was learning about Kirby's story, his daughter, Kate, who has Down syndrome, came onto the screen and was visibly upset about something. I watched Kirby focus his attention on his daughter and have a conversation with her for a couple of minutes that helped meet her needs, then we continued our call. It was a great moment to see where Kirby puts his priorities today.

Over time, as you seek worth through the approval and acceptance of others, you lose a bit of your own identity. You forget who you are and focus only on trying to achieve that next accolade. Eventually, it becomes exhausting. You no longer know what you believe in. Your worth is being driven by the next thing that you accomplish. And, of course, if you don't accomplish it, well, then you're not worthy.

"What's at the end of that rainbow you are chasing?"
–Nick Soman, founder and CEO, Decent

When I was in my second year of business school at Harvard, I got a second bout of Guillain-Barré syndrome, which meant I was paralyzed. I wasn't able to walk. I spent time in intensive care. I would need to learn to walk again. While all of my friends were getting awesome jobs, I was lying in bed. I couldn't talk. I couldn't move. I was angry. I thought I was going to die.

I thankfully recovered and moved to Seattle to work for Amazon. And after a year, I left because I had visions of starting a company, but I didn't know what I was going to do. But I was single and lonely and thought, *Hey, maybe I can crack this dating thing.* It was an interesting ride, one that had a lot of struggle, but I didn't feel alive in this pursuit. This problem did not need my brain. It felt frivolous. I was lost. Was this really a problem worth solving? As one of my favorite poets, Rainer Maria Rilke, said, "The purpose of life is to be defeated by greater and greater things." I certainly felt defeated. I hadn't found my zone.

And so I thought deeply about the next thing I wanted to do. I didn't care if it was going to make me the most successful entrepreneur or not. I wanted to make sure it was about more than me; that win or lose, I was going to be grateful for the journey. I wanted to tackle a hard problem, but not one where I had to prove that there was a market opportunity. So I leaned into another personal problem I faced (not dating–I was married now), and that was providing more-affordable health insurance for Americans.

For the first time, I felt connected to a purpose that was so much bigger than me, and it wasn't about the money. It wasn't about the outcome. It wasn't about the approval of others. I realized, *If I do this right, well, I get to keep doing it.* And the clarity of purpose to provide more-affordable health insurance sparked a series of lucky opportunities to build a great team and to raise money from top-tier investors. I let go of my ego, which was interfering with my inner compass. I knew there was no way that I could do this myself. I embraced humility. And I stumbled into a realization that if I'm going to spend a lot of my life at work, then I need to make sure I'm fully engaged, and that it is work worth doing. I have finally arrived at a place where I am in integrity with who and where I want to be in my life, and I don't need approval from others.

In many ways, my paralysis was a gift. Sure, it got me thinking about the precious value of time. But I also reflect on what life would be like if I got exactly what I was working so hard to achieve in my early start-up days. Really, what's at the end of that rainbow you are chasing? And if that outcome feels really satisfying to you, then you're probably on the right track. If you don't know how it would feel, you might be on the wrong track, and then you'll have an opportunity to create a new goal worth chasing. Just make sure it's your own.

Whatever Happens Is Perfect (WHIP)

What happens is as it is meant to be. The future is never prescriptive. It is all make-believe. So when the future comes to pass, the only benchmark is what you thought would happen. But what you thought would happen is simply in your imagination. What happens if you let that go? What if the things that happen are exactly the things that were supposed to happen? It's not good or bad. It just is. Focus on the intention. Let go of the outcome.

Who would you be without that outcome? Is it scary? Does it feel empty—or is it empowering? When my wife and I took this approach and made the decision to move abroad, it was like our entire world changed. The experiences were so new that we didn't try to manufacture an expectation. Whatever happens is going to be perfect.

It was perfect when we got two flat tires on the side of the road and couldn't get the spare on. It was perfect when we didn't have a place to live but were confident we'd find something. It was perfect when we tried to cross the border into Panama and had no idea where we were supposed to go. Yes, of course it was a little stressful, but these were all interesting micro-challenges, and we knew we would figure it out. We could get worked up about it and pissed off and frustrated, but that wouldn't change the outcome.

And so, "Whatever happens is perfect" (WHIP) became our new mantra. And when the chips were down or we were getting stressed out (with each other or our circumstance), we'd look at each other and say, "Whatever happens is perfect," and that would be our cue to ease up and WHIP it!

Think back to the recent past when something went wrong for you. Maybe it was an argument with your spouse, an injury, a deal that you were working on that didn't close. Congratulations! Now think about how that setback was actually your ally. Why was it perfect? What did it reveal that you can learn about yourself? How was it all meant to be? These are the learning moments, and you can either embrace them or resist. WHIP it!

Be Bold

Boldness is a willingness to listen to your intuition and follow it even if it goes against common beliefs. It may not be popular. Heck, it might feel a little reckless. But that all-too-familiar feeling of hesitation is deep seated. It originates in our reptilian brain, warning us to avoid danger. It is reinforced by friends and family who tell us to play it safe. Cultural building blocks also encourage us to play the safe card (get a safe job so I can get health-care benefits and secure a mortgage to buy a house so that I need to keep my safe job in order to pay that mortgage). When we create an environment that energizes us, taking a leap doesn't feel as risky.

"When you see a problem, well . . . fix it."
—Madeline Haydon, founder and CEO, nutpods

I wanted to build a brand that felt more authentic than the processed creamers out there. I was working at a nonprofit before starting nutpods. I didn't have the nondairy creamer or consumer packaged goods experience coursing through my veins. I just wanted something that was a better option for people like me, without all the processed sugars. And so I leapt to see if I could do it.

It was hard. I am a female. I am a woman of color. I grew up with Vietnamese parents, and the feeling was that it's less about who you are and more about what you achieve. The common question was whether I would go into business or medicine. The expectation was a good job for survivability and sustainability. But as a product of Vietnamese refugees and someone who fought my way to navigate with English as a second language, I was always scrappy. And that scrappiness drove me to take the leap and build nutpods.

Being bold requires a critical ingredient: uncertainty. You don't know what you don't know. That's the portal you are going through to introduce new energy into your life. It is the very act of entering the unknown that reveals a new possibility. Being bold is having the courage to face that uncertainty and work with it to harness what it is trying to teach you and give you. If you knew the outcome, you wouldn't need to be bold.

One of the most inspiring stories of being bold and leaning into uncertainty is what Fran Dunaway and Naomi Gonzalez did when they started TomboyX. Talk about being bold. Fran was fifty-five when she started the company. This was a leap into an uncertain world—and now her world has changed forever.

"We didn't know a knit from a woven or P&L from a balance sheet."
–Fran Dunaway, TomboyX

You know, it was really interesting because Naomi and I are both fixers, and I was just frustrated because I wanted a cool shirt like a Robert Graham or Ben Sherman but made for a woman's body. I mean, seriously, you could go into the men's department and find these beautiful shirts that were beautiful fabrics, and when you go into the women's section it was crappy fabrics and it had flowers or, you know, pastels and just not–they didn't have any fun details under the collar. So, it was really the craving for that kind of a product that was the impetus for the business.

We picked the name TomboyX because we thought it was a cute name. We both identified as tomboys, and it was kind of that nod to the masculine influence on the shirts. But it was interesting because during the Kickstarter campaign, we launched a Kickstarter to put our shirts into production. And it was during that campaign that the name was resonating in a very powerful way that people knew immediately. It was instant brand recognition. And if you think about it, other than, like, 1-800-Flowers, most company names have to build what it means.

We just lucked out that we got the trademark for Tomboy and TomboyX. And so, that was a really interesting moment, because my background has been in politics, and it was about a week into the Kickstarter campaign when we thought, *Gosh, this is really resonating in a powerful way.* And then we almost felt a responsibility to solve that problem for our community because there were a lot of people like us that had never been seen or heard in the fashion industry. And we had a lot of very specific needs and wants. And so, that was where the fixers in us kicked in and kind of took it on as a responsibility to figure out what the hell we had and then what to do with it. Because honestly, we didn't know a knit from a woven or P&L from a balance sheet, so we had a lot to learn.

Exercise: Finding and Creating Your Energy

Close your eyes and think about those environments where you get the most energy. For me it was living in Costa Rica. Maybe for you it is doing yoga or being on a road trip. Write down the top three feelings that you experience when you think about those environments.

1. ______________
2. ______________
3. ______________

Think about the three people in your life that give you the most energy. It doesn't have to be people you see all the time, but those that fill you with energy whenever you see them. Write down how they make you feel.

1. ____________________

2. ____________________

3. ____________________

Now, think about those same three people. What is it about their energy that you are attracted to? What do they do that draws you to them?

1. ____________________

2. ____________________

3. ____________________

This is a simple exercise that is all about triggers. So often, our ability to attract more energy is about being in the right mind-set to receive it. The actual environments and people create the recall for us, wherever we may be. The work ahead involves managing your mind-set to get energy even if you are not in your high-energy environment, which most of us aren't most of the time.

HARNESS ENERGY
CHAPTER SUMMARY

Energy represents the inputs of creation. Anything that is built requires energy to fashion it in a way that will serve a purpose. Your life is no different. In this chapter, we discussed how to think about energy and how to harness it in your design. Here are the key takeaways:

- Energy is what gives us the ability to do work.
- Energy comes from the environment, both your physical surroundings as well as people and resources.
- Your physical environment can have a profound impact on your energy level.
- Maximizing your energy is holding on to the feeling created by energizing experiences, regardless of where you are and who you are surrounded by.
- The more energy you emit for others, the more you receive in return.
- When you are clear on intention, you will maximize energy because it has a purpose.
- Your available energy will go first to neutralize the things that drain you versus accelerating your growth.
- Opening yourself to new energy comes from:
  - Focusing on inputs.
  - Letting go of shame.
  - Seeking approval from within.
  - Reminding yourself that "Whatever happens is perfect."
  - Being bold.

HARNESS ENERGY
CHAPTER SUMMARY

The Exercise in This Chapter

- Finding and Creating Your Energy

Highlighted Designers

- The Drive to Change Our Environment
  —Russell Benaroya
- The Disease to Please
  —Casey Roloff
- "If it's good enough for Jay-Z, well. . . ."
  —Max Nelson
- "Nobody cares as much about me as I think they do."
  —Kirby Winfield
- "What's at the end of that rainbow you are chasing?"
  —Nick Soman
- "When you see a problem, well . . . fix it."
  —Madeline Haydon
- "We didn't know a knit from a woven or P&L from a balance sheet."
  —Fran Dunaway

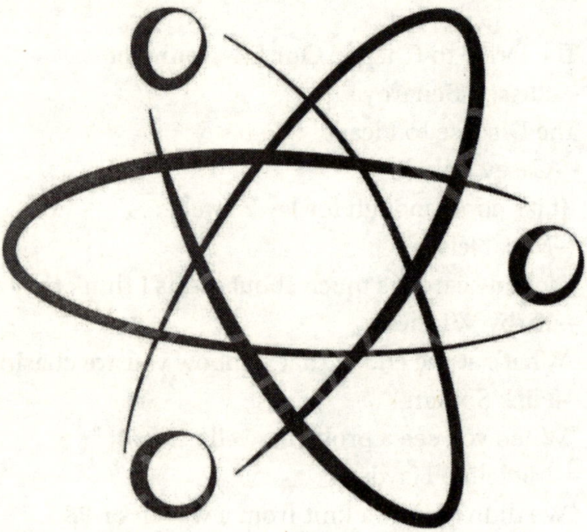

STEP 4: GET IN AND STAY IN YOUR GENIUS ZONE

"My genius zone was harder to find than somebody's genius zone who's really good at taking SATs and is really good at solving analytical problems. My genius zone is recognizing talent and surrounding myself with people that are better than I am."

—Matt Oppenheimer, cofounder and CEO, Remitly

I first learned about the idea of the genius zone back in 2012. I was running a technology company called EveryMove and working with my business coach Lex Sisney, author of *Organizational Physics*. Part of his process is to help you identify your genius zone and architect your life so that you can spend at least 80 percent of your time in it. Your genius zone is that unique power you have where you feel most alive, where the work feels effortless, and where you perform better than most.

I didn't know my genius zone—I had never thought about it before. I essentially spent all my days running around, scattered, trying to plug holes to keep the start-up ship afloat. What I didn't realize was that the very behavior of trying to keep everything on course was a contributor to things being off-course. I was sticking my nose and fingers into areas where I didn't have expertise and certainly didn't have genius. I had a hard time teasing out where my role as CEO aligned with flexing my innate talent for what the company needed.

My biggest blocker was control and the desire to maintain it. I was clouded by control masked as wanting to help other people get their job done . . . and not even help people get their job done, but kind of do it for them, or have it done in the way I would do it. It is suffocating just writing this. I was the CEO of a business who wanted to control areas of the organization that I was not an expert in, *and* I wanted to spend time doing other people's jobs that I *hired them to do* because of their innate expertise in that area.

I was far outside of my genius zone.

When I interviewed Nick Soman from Decent, he shared something that really helped me appreciate the power of the genius zone.

"Staying in my genius zone by helping others stay in theirs."
—Nick Soman, founder and CEO, Decent

When I started Decent, I took a page out of Fred Wilson's "What a CEO Does" playbook, which was (i) set the overall vision and strategy for the company, (ii) recruit, hire, and retain the best talent, and (iii) make sure there is always enough cash in the bank. Delegate everything else. I am certainly competent in many areas of business, and sure, sometimes I like the idea of taking a deep dive into figuring out some growth hack to acquire more customers, but I am uniquely skilled at leading what has converged to create this company. And it is so satisfying.

I charted the vision to provide more-affordable health insurance, and my team responded. They moved mountains and launched a product in less than a year. They did everything they wanted to do, and I did everything I wanted to do. We closed a round of financing with a top-tier investor, and I have been lucky enough to bring on and retain some incredible industry experts. Staying humble and creating the vehicle for others to be in their zone of genius is what is enabling me to stay in mine.

Nick taught me something here that may not be obvious. My first takeaway was that, of course, if I'm the CEO, then I should resist the temptation to venture into areas outside of what I am uniquely positioned to do. That is why I hire great people: to be in their genius zone. It's not only disrespectful but also demotivating to infringe on others' work. That's good learning for sure. But what Nick had me consider even further was, if I'm consistently drawn to, excel at, and get joy from working in areas that don't match the areas of responsibility of the CEO, then maybe the CEO role isn't the best role for me in that circumstance.

Life design is not about aspiring to the top job in an organization. Life design doesn't care about titles. When you let go of the desire for status and focus on your own road map instead, can't you feel the pressure around you lighten up?

It may explain why, today, in another company that I cofounded, I'm not the CEO. In fact, my partner is a much better CEO for that type of business than I would be. The irony is that in the last business we built together as partners, I was the CEO. It wasn't until I could finally let go of status and realize that my priority is getting and staying in my genius zone that things got a whole lot easier.

DEFINING THE GENIUS ZONE

Your zone of genius is your unique power. It is at the intersection of what you are uniquely talented at and where you get the most energy. It is where you are taking advantage of your natural talents and are in an area that you truly enjoy. Being there almost feels like it gives you an unfair advantage. Gay Hendricks, a well-known social psychologist, coined the term *zone of genius* in his 2010 book *The Big Leap.*

How do you know when you're in your zone of genius? Ask yourself these five questions:

1. What comes naturally to you?
2. When do people say, "Wow, how did you do that?"
3. What are you doing when you lose track of time?
4. What are you doing when you feel most accomplished?
5. What do you do such that when you're done, you feel even more energized?

Sounds pretty awesome, right? Who wouldn't want to spend their time in their genius zone? So why don't we all spend our time in our genius zone? Here are three reasons:

1. We don't do the work to define our genius zone, so we aren't intentional about it.

2. We are scared that our genius zone isn't valued, so we keep it suppressed.
3. We compromise our life design formula and accept our circumstances, sacrificing the opportunity to spend time in our genius zone.

YOUR GENIUS ZONE AND YOUR BUSINESS

The work environment asks important questions that relate to the genius zone equation. And those are:

1. Is your genius zone fulfilling a function that the organization needs right now; and
2. What is the value the business is willing to assign to it?

When your genius zone is aligned with what an organization needs, and they value that contribution in terms of compensation, then you are well aligned in the workplace and can thrive. If those elements do not align, if your genius zone is not fulfilling an important role *or* it's not that highly valued, then it may be a good indication that you are in the wrong environment.

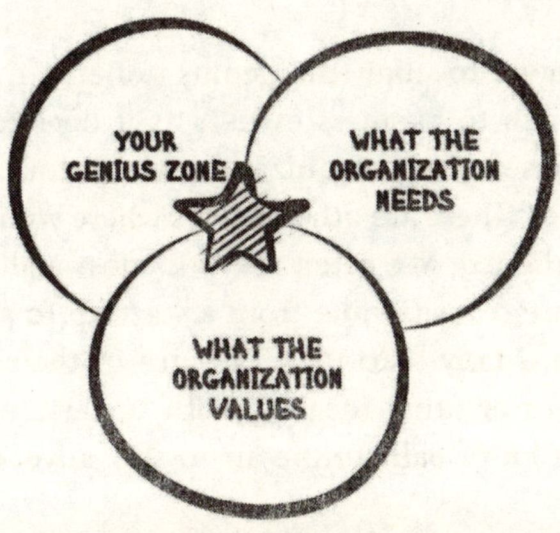

What I love about bringing a genius-zone perspective to the work environment is that it is not emotional. We often so desperately want to be valued, and when we are not, we get really upset or angry and act out in ways that drain our energy and that of our organizations. But in designing your life, you dictate the environment that will best support your genius zone. If you're not in it, rather than try to bend the environment to your will, change it.

Your responsibility is to continue seeking clarity about your zone of genius by learning how to apply your seemingly effortless work to a need in the world. Great organizations (and, more often, great managers) may also help you do that because they're invested in your personal development. Most won't. Many of us end up thrashing around for a long time, hoping that the organization will finally see the value in what we have to provide.

What if you were more honest with yourself and those around you about your genius zone? Think how much freer you would feel in your life if you weren't slogging away at something that doesn't map to your genius zone. It may take some time to really figure out how to best apply your genius zone, and that might mean you accept positions or opportunities that you come to find out are not a match. No problem. That's the journey, and it can be approached in a lighthearted, experimental way.

The struggle to align the genius zone in the workplace applies as much to business owners as it does to employees. There are phases of an organization where your genius zone may be perfect. There are other phases where your genius zone may be misaligned. We often see this most acutely for companies that are transitioning from a start-up to a more stable growth stage. Many start-up CEOs are in their genius zone when they are creating, dealing with uncertainty, and having to keep a lot of balls in the air to stay alive. But when an organization begins to get traction and roles have to become more defined, those very same CEOs feel like they're in a strait-jacket or can't stand the idea of spending more time coaching instead of doing.

One of the best things you can do as part of your life design is make sure that your genius zone is aligned with an environment that values your contribution. That does not always have to be about money, either. Value can come from how and where you contribute to the community. Value can be how you and a partner divide responsibilities at home. Value can be your side hustle, or something you are working on outside of work hours. When you know your genius zone, it's a lot easier to both assess your current environment and evaluate new opportunities.

DO THE WORK TO FIND YOUR GENIUS ZONE

You may already know your genius zone. Most of us have to unpack it under a mountain of other responsibilities we have caked on to our lives. When you don't spend very much time in your genius zone, it is hard to recognize. If you have snuffed it out because you perceive that the world doesn't value it, then it's like a muscle that can atrophy over time. Your genius zone isn't so innate that you can ignore it without exercising it. Sure, it doesn't hurt to start off with a natural talent. Michael Phelps was already predisposed to being a great swimmer. Kilian Jornet is one of the world's elite ultrarunners and not only has the right physique for running but also grew up in the high-altitude Spanish Alps.

Genius zones show up all over the place—but the responsibility is to find yours and spend as much time in it as possible.

Exercise: Find Your Genius Zone

Inspired by Gay Hendricks and his book *The Big Leap*, here is a simple exercise to get you oriented to your zone of genius. This series of questions is designed to get to the heart of your genius. Consider having a close friend ask you these questions and maybe you do the same for them. It's always easier when you're expressing your responses out loud or on paper rather than mulling them in your head.

1. What do you most love to do?
2. What are your unique abilities?
3. When do people make comments about how "amazing" you are at something?
4. Where do you get the most satisfaction at work, especially satisfaction that is also acknowledged frequently by others?
5. Where do you lose track of time?

There is another model that I really like. Josh Steimle, in *The 7 Systems of Influence*, drafted a fun way of finding your genius zone. Give this one a try:

List your zones of expertise. These are not where you are the best or the most knowledgeable but where you are an expert because you have some unique experience. This could be based on where you live, your degree, experiences you have had, etc. There are no boundaries when thinking about your expertise. List them here:

1. ______	6. ______	11. ______
2. ______	7. ______	12. ______
3. ______	8. ______	13. ______
4. ______	9. ______	14. ______
5. ______	10. ______	15. ______

Next, start overlapping your areas of expertise. You might overlap two or more areas. It is the combination of your unique capabilities that creates a genius zone, something hard for others to replicate. Sure, they may be able to replicate one of your abilities, but when you draw on multiple aspects that create your superpower, it will be unique.

For example, consider a biology major with corporate finance experience who lived in Africa, speaks three languages, and runs ultramarathons. Each one of these is a special attribute or experience. How might they overlap to define a genius zone? Your genius zone could be microfinance in developing countries, or cross-border consulting. Who knows? It could be less work-specific and more about how you are adept at understanding people and connecting with them deeply. This exercise is a creative endeavor. Not all your combos will be practical for you. You just may not be able to prioritize some combinations right now, or they might not be something that the marketplace values at the level you require.

Discovering your genius zone is not a science. It is an experiment. Remember, think in terms of experiments. Try it on. See how it feels. Learn and iterate.

ACKNOWLEDGE YOUR ANTI-GENIUS ZONE

It is often easier to think about your anti-genius zone rather than to define your genius zone. You definitely know what you *don't* love to do, where you *don't* have unique abilities, and where you *aren't* satisfied. In order to create the essential space to operate inside your genius zone, you are going to have to make room by getting rid of things that aren't in your genius zone. We're not just talking about your activities at work, either. Think about all areas of your life, even some that feel like they are your nonnegotiable responsibility (e.g., mowing the lawn, doing laundry, washing dishes, transporting kids). It's all on the table.

Exercise: Find Your Anti-Genius Zone

1. What do you **least** love to do?
2. What do you do that does **not** leverage your unique abilities?
3. What produces the **least** amount of satisfaction for you in relation to the time you spend doing it?

Just getting these ideas on paper is a big win. It is cathartic to express your genius zone and anti-genius zone, because then you can start to do something with them. Here are a couple of considerations for action you can take now:

1. *Communicate* your anti-genius zone. If you don't let people know where you feel least distinctive

or capable or satisfied, they aren't going to be able to help you make changes. These people may be your manager, your board of directors, or your spouse or partner. It is on you to communicate, and too often we don't. We suck it up, take it on, wear the martyr badge, and hope that people are going to acknowledge our sacrifice and reward us for it. They won't. If you are proactive about communicating your anti-genius zone, most people will be receptive to supporting you in shifting away from it. Don't hope they do. Ask them to. Be clear.

2. *Delegate.* Business leadership is about getting the right people in the right roles at the right time. It is about *not* doing things yourself, because you have people on your team with a genius zone that is complementary to your own. If you don't delegate work to people that are better equipped to do it than you, you're harming yourself and doing a disservice to your team members. When you take on work that is not in your genius zone when there is someone better able to accomplish it, your leadership suffers. Before diving into that next responsibility, ask yourself, "Could someone else do this as well as or better than me?"

It is crucial to remember that your time is valuable. The value of your time is the cost of not being in your genius zone, and that is hugely expensive in your life design.

"Noses in. Fingers out."
–Russell Benaroya

In 2004, I was a bright-eyed entrepreneur who thought that starting and running a company couldn't be that hard. I had seen others crush it that I thought were far less capable than me, so I should be able to do it as well, right? The best MBA you can get might be the one where you get thrown into the fire of running a start-up, because that's when you really get tested. I was going to do whatever it took to make this healthcare business successful.

But I realized that, over time, I was crippling the progress of the business, because I had my hands in areas that were already being managed by people I had hired. I would spend late nights going through and reconciling patient balances. I would build spreadsheets with all kinds of formulas designed to answer some pretty basic business performance questions. I'm not suggesting that these weren't useful exercises, but is this what the CEO should be spending their time doing? Was this my genius zone? Was I effectively empowering the people to be their best? Probably not.

Sandra Rorem, a member of our board of directors, gave me some great advice. She said, "Great leaders keep their noses in and their fingers out." My job was to figure out what needed doing, put the right people with the right genius zones in the right roles, let them execute, and figure out which obstacles I needed to break down to help them succeed.

If you're wondering what this has to do with the genius zone, the answer is: everything. If you desire to spend a majority of your time in your genius zone, you have to figure out how to stop doing things that are not in your genius zone, even if you are competent at them.

When I was in the TechStars accelerator program in Seattle with Matt Oppenheimer, the cofounder and CEO of Remitly, a billion-dollar global mobile payments company changing the lives of people around the world, I admired Matt from Day One. His stoic disposition. His clear focus. He was someone that I knew would make something happen. What Matt shared with me is a great example of what I mean by genius zone.

"I'm the person who knows the person who has the answer."

–Matt Oppenheimer, cofounder and CEO, Remitly

I spent a number of years before and after business school at jobs that I didn't really love, but I was still learning. I'm not a big believer in leading life from the principle of "Endure this dissatisfaction now for a future passion," but I did and I'm glad I did. I was starting to really home in on what I was uniquely good at. Once I realized that, I was ready to leave Barclays, where I was running mobile banking in Kenya, and begin what has become Remitly.

I realized that I'm just not the smartest person in the room. I feel lucky that I got into Dartmouth and went to Harvard Business School, but I'm by no means the cream of the crop when it comes to solving hard problems. Give me the mission to lead a team, inspire a group, raise capital, or communicate a vision, and I'll do that all day. The challenge I have always had is *How do I articulate that capability?* It's a little soft. How do you really articulate that superpower?

Society puts a lot of value on high intellect, entrance exam scores, and grades. I didn't really have those, so in high school I was actually pretty insecure. But the one thing I was uniquely good at was getting a group to follow me, to believe in me. That's my genius zone. Getting into a good college created the space for me to shore up my academics, and that helped a lot. I continued to seek opportunities that would round out my capabilities, but I was pretty clear where I achieved outsized returns.

It is why, when I started Remitly, I found someone to work with who is off-the-charts IQ smart and one of the best problem solvers I know. My genius zone requires that I surround myself with people in areas where I am weaker, and I am good at recognizing talent. It's so liberating. I don't feel like I need to be the person that knows the answer. My genius zone is that I'm the person who knows the person who has the answer.

What I love about Matt's experience is that his genius zone wasn't obvious for a long time. It was easy to resist because it didn't feel tangible enough. When he finally embraced it, things got lighter and easier. His honesty allowed him to more easily resource for those areas not in his genius zone.

We talked earlier about Madeline Haydon and her bold bet to harness her energy and build nutpods. She is also someone who might argue that her genius zone isn't quite as obvious, but she too has embraced it. Now, her genius zone is part of the integral fabric of what makes nutpods so special. For Madeline, the most important benefit of knowing her genius zone is knowing her anti-genius zone.

"I am the storyteller."
–Madeline Haydon, founder and CEO, nutpods

My unique super ability is that people like me, and that was hard to own. I have so many smart people around me. My husband is an investment banker and super-data driven. And then there is Madeline. "She is so nice. She is so caring." How is that a genius zone?

What I realized is that this translates into an important business benefit, like the ability to build teams. People are attracted to the work that I am doing and want to help me, even if I can't afford to pay them. I'm the storyteller that can translate a vision into something real for team members, investors, board members, and trade and marketing partners. I care less if our trade spend decreases by 1.4 percent and care more about the team's needs and creating great new products that fill a market gap. I am sure we have some target for freight spend and profitability, but that drains my energy. I have hired a great team for that expertise. And when I feel insecure about being nice and caring, I see how people react to that authenticity and their desire to want to see this business succeed. Investors and customers ultimately connect with stories. My genius zone is building that bridge.

Finding your genius zone isn't automatic. It may come from the struggle of experimenting in a number of roles. It may be someone telling you that you need to move on and try something else. That's what happened for Sharelle, and she's glad it did.

"Eventually, he fired me."

—Sharelle Klaus, CEO and founder, DRY Soda Company

My genius zone *aha* moment came before I became an entrepreneur and started DRY Soda. I was working in consulting and on a public works project. I was struggling and not enjoying myself. The one thing I really enjoyed was building the relationships with the client and selling our services.

I remember my boss coming in one day and telling me how he thought I really needed to be in business development. *No way,* I thought. *That's not real work. I can do the spreadsheet stuff.* I was hurt that he didn't seem to value the work that I was doing even though I wasn't loving the work. (I know: Twisted, right?) Eventually, he fired me. Yes, he fired me and told me that I needed to move on. I got a new job working in consulting at Price Waterhouse. And guess what I was doing? Yes, business development.

GET IN AND STAY IN YOUR GENIUS ZONE

CHAPTER SUMMARY

Connecting to your genius zone is an essential design principle. It will significantly reduce the amount of energy drain that keeps you from moving forward at the pace and in the direction that you desire. The most important thing you can do is start defining your genius zone, followed by assessing how your environment supports or detracts from it. Some key points from this chapter include:

- Your genius zone represents your unique superpower and sits at the intersection of what you are uniquely good at and what gives you energy.
- Most of us spend too little time in our genius zone, and that keeps us from realizing our possibilities.
- Your genius zone may be in conflict with your current business environment, and that is an opportunity to reassess. If your genius zone is not valued, you will not be driven to grow.
- Knowing your anti-genius zone is just as important in creating the space to design the life you want.

GET IN AND STAY IN YOUR GENIUS ZONE
CHAPTER SUMMARY

Exercises in This Chapter

- Find Your Genius Zone
- Find Your Anti-Genius Zone

Highlighted Designers

- "Staying in my genius zone by helping others stay in theirs."
  —Nick Soman
- "Noses in. Fingers out."
  —Russell Benaroya
- "I'm the person who knows the person who has the answer."
  —Matt Oppenheimer
- "I am the storyteller."
  —Madeline Haydon
- "Eventually, he fired me."
  —Sharelle Klaus

STEP 5: TAKE ACTION

"And it's crazy. Over and over and over again, everyone said, 'You're doing what? You're nuts.' And you know what? I'm a problem solver."

—Lori Torres, founder and CEO, Parcel Pending

"But you know, for me, it just became crystal clear that I'm definitely going to die. I may not even have that long on this earth, and so I don't want to waste my time."

—Nick Soman, founder and CEO, Decent

Taking action is an obvious, but generally not well-executed, component of life design, because we are masters at procrastination. There are a lot of *what ifs,* and *I should haves,* and *I could nevers,* and it's amazing how few of us take decisive action in the direction that we want to move. Instead, we let the environment around us dictate our path, which feels pretty comfortable because we are going with the flow. We don't disrupt the status quo. Relationships are maintained. Our jobs are steady. Everything is kind of . . . fine. And we're secretly pissed at ourselves because the one thing we simply can't control is time, and that keeps marching right along, even though we haven't taken action.

Every action is a learning opportunity that will give you some feedback. Think of actions as experiments you can run to test your principles. We are all works in progress, so there doesn't need to be the expectation that an action will lead to a certain outcome. Do not think of action as a culmination once you have figured it out. Rather, actions are the micro things you do to achieve your life design.

The first step to take action is to verbalize your new reality: "I am in control of designing my life." It is simple but profound. When I finally started believing that, I became aware of how much control I gave to others and to the circumstances around me. The challenge is that it's not easy to see, because things seem to be going OK: a family, a job, friends, a home in a nice neighborhood. But it felt like everything that had happened just kind of happened. It is so easy to traverse life as the product of the wants, needs, and desires of others. It can happen on a personal level, on a professional level, and on an institutional level. People want you to act a certain way because it's safe and predictable. But what if that's in conflict with the foundation of the life you want to design: your principles, energy, and genius zone?

Action is not running off and quitting your job and moving to Costa Rica. Well, let me correct myself here. That might actually be what you do, but the action should be the result of a process of figuring out what problem it is solving for you. The definition of *action* is the ability to turn your life design into reality.

ACTION IS DISRUPTIVE

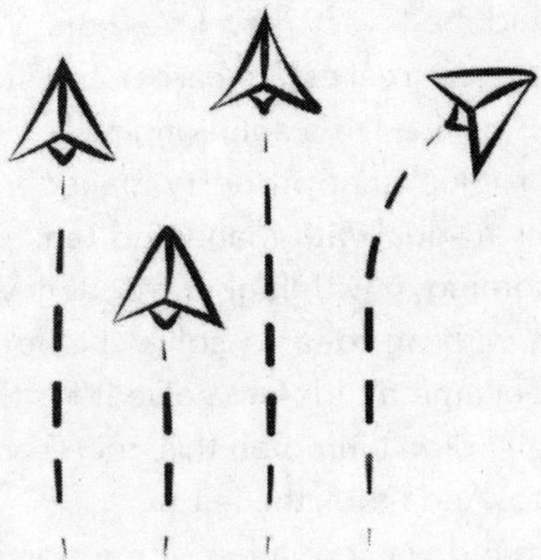

Don't think for a second that taking action is a pleasant, smooth ride. It's not. Someone is probably going to be upset with you. Someone will likely try to convince you not to do it. The transition to living your principles, to being in integrity, to taking control of your life is going to rock the status quo. If it feels uncomfortable, then you're probably on the right track.

There is no transformation if you continue doing what you have always done. Don't be fooled into believing that safety means staying put, comfortable with what you know. Not today. If we have learned anything, it is that there are no guarantees for any of us. Don't be lulled into complacency. You have the capability. You know how to run the experiments. You know that you are going to figure it out. Of course things aren't going to go exactly as you planned. Your life is not designed for perfectly orchestrated plans. It is designed for resilience.

"Everyone told me I was crazy. Like, nuts."
–Lori Torres, founder and CEO, Parcel Pending

Everyone told me I was crazy. Like, nuts. Why would I leave a thirty-year real estate career and start a locker company? Because I'm a solution finder first, and the really big problem that property managers were facing was how to deal with managing tenant packages that were coming in with higher frequency. And what started out with an idea to solve this for the Irvine Company became an idea to solve it for the industry as a whole. If I didn't jump on this, then someone else was going to. And I took the leap.

My husband was not a fan of me doing this (side note: we are not married today). I was the breadwinner of our household. He wanted me to get a job. So I went out and interviewed and got three offers immediately. I thought that if I could do that, then I was going to start this company and my fallback would be . . . a job.

The instinct for action started from a young age. I had a lot of responsibilities and started working early. When someone tells me I can't do something, well . . . I just might do it. I didn't go to college. I have a high school diploma, and I worked my way up to SVP in a billion-dollar company in an environment where I was told I wouldn't make VP. Game on.

Of course, there are moments after taking a leap when you freak out, but that's just expected. I remember driving down the 405 freeway and thinking, *Oh my God, this is so hard. I don't know if I can do this, I don't know if I can do this.* And I read something about manufacturing, because I knew nothing about manufacturing and I knew nothing about technology. And so here I'm dealing with China and issues in China and thinking, *If I don't get this figured out, I don't have a business. I got to get lockers.*

But there are two things that really turn action into impact. The first is that I'm a planner. I had a road map for Parcel Pending from Day One. I knew where I wanted to go. I focused on executing the plan. I'm so convinced that our success was because we had a plan. And we checked in on that plan, and we talked about it. It's like, *OK, where are you at? What is supposed to be accomplished by this point?* And when you have that clear plan, I think you can accomplish anything. Anything.

The second thing is that I'm not afraid to ask for help. I don't have an ego around it. We had to manufacture these lockers. What did I know about manufacturing? I never knew how to raise money. So I just started talking to people, and one call grew into many more, and I built trusting relationships and wasn't afraid to show that I didn't know what I was doing.

We sold the business eighteen to twenty-four months before we thought we would. Neopost knocked on our door. I told them that we weren't in a position to sell because we didn't think we'd get full value. They were not deterred. They wanted to close in six weeks. We announced the sale of the company on January 31, 2019, for $100 million.

ACTION IS ACCEPTING FEAR

One pro tip is that it is OK to be afraid when taking action on your life design. In fact, it is often essential and unavoidable. Fear is an emotion that you feel when encountering a threat. You can't help it. We all know the feeling. The fear of that upcoming test, difficult conversation with a friend, or new project you have been assigned and have no idea how to tackle.

Fear is deeply embedded in us because it keeps us safe. Fear is an absolutely reasonable emotion when faced with bold action. It is also the precursor to courage. Fear can be a motivating driver to take action, or it can tie you up in knots, paralyzing you. Courage is what you do when you feel fear. How do you want to harness your fear to find your courage?

"I made fear my ally."
–Max Nelson, founder and CEO, HOOD

I finally got to a point where I just started believing in the purposeful nature of the universe and radically accepted it. The truth is that I got sober. I had a drug problem. And I finally accepted my fear, and rather than dull that emotion, I used it to catapult me into a journey of walking through the doors that are open instead of pounding down the ones that are closed. It may sound a little counterintuitive. Entrepreneurs are supposed to do whatever it takes, right? I was supposed to make sure that I could do anything to get Jay-Z to put on one of our hats, get photographed, and put it on Instagram, right?

I just let go of being scared, accepted the fear, and realized that every day is going to be another set of interesting challenges where something is going to happen, and I'll manage through it. Our motto at HOOD is "Never leave it behind." We make hats where people put the name of their neighborhood on it, so that makes sense. But for me, "Never leave it behind" is also about not forgetting what I have gone through to get to this point. Now I'm seeing some success, and I have a choice. I can either let my fear drive me to worry about when the other shoe is going to drop and what is going to go wrong next. Or, I can use fear to remind me of what I have overcome and that where I am is exactly where I am meant to be.

Fear is a powerful force for action, which can be managed by having a plan to act. Action and planning are intimately connected through fear. Fear can be a huge motivation. I have a fear that if we don't move now we're going to miss the opportunity. I have a fear that our most valuable resource is our team of people, but our culture prevents them from thriving.

In fact, Tim Ferriss, the author of many books, including *Tools of Titans* and *The 4-Hour Workweek*, promotes a framework called fear-setting. The basic idea is to use fear to drive the creation of a plan that will mitigate the risks of an unappealing outcome coming to pass. So, let's talk about the power of a plan.

ACTION REQUIRES PLANNING TO ACT

I have a good friend, Andrew Sykes, who practices in the world of behavioral science and understanding why people do what they do. A number of years ago, when I owned a health technology company, we were talking about why it is so hard for people to stop doing things that everyone knows are unhealthy (e.g., smoking and eating poorly). He shared a behavioral science concept with me called hyperbolic discounting.

Hyperbolic discounting refers to the tendency of people to choose a smaller, short-term reward rather than a larger, later reward. In other words, we like immediate pleasure (a good burger or a smoke) and discount the value of the long-term payoff (e.g., a longer life). No surprise, right? It is common to struggle with delayed gratification. Life design isn't about what you are going to consume today or tomorrow, but rather the long-term path you commit to pave for yourself. And that, my friends, takes planning.

"Optimism is not a plan."
–David Nilssen, cofounder and CEO, Guidant Financial

My partner, Jeremy Ames, and I started Guidant Financial in 2003 and today have helped over 21,000 people open small businesses in the United States. We do this by helping entrepreneurs unlock their regulated retirement accounts to put them toward starting a company. We then help them ensure that those funds are properly accounted for in order to stay in compliance with the relevant tax exemptions for retirement savings. Pretty cool, right?

But it hasn't always been so rosy. In fact, in the financial crisis of 2008–2009, we nearly lost everything as the economy sputtered and regulations threatened our entire business model. The writing was on the wall for us beginning in 2007, but we invested unabated in big enterprise software, hiring executive management, and bloating payroll in the hope that things were going to be OK. They weren't. In October 2008, we began what would result in three layoff rounds, going from 115 to 30 employees and being in debt over a million dollars. As I like to joke, "We were so broke that we didn't even have enough money to declare bankruptcy."

I reflect on that time, and we knew intuitively we needed to do something, but we knew it was easier for us to err on the side of what was easier at the moment. And wow, it created some serious downstream problems. And this error rocked me for a long time. It was also compounded by my own insecurity at not having gone to college, starting this business when I was barely twenty-five years old, and feeling like an impostor for much of my time in leadership.

I got caught up in constantly questioning my own judgment and feeling insecure about my intuition. I almost let optimism kill the business in 2008, and I'm not doing that today. When the pandemic hit, we had a plan and took action, engaging the team to protect our people and continue serving our clients. This included radically reducing expenses.

I'm still an anxious person today (as you would be able to tell if you saw my nails—or lack of them), but I know how I need to process information to get things out and work with my partner to figure out the right plan together. I don't withhold in the hope that things will get better.

We learned the hard way about that.

The whole point of designing a life that you want to live is that you actually have to design it. Design is about planning and envisioning the world as you want to navigate through it. We love the idea of the finished product, but so many of us struggle with taking the time to go through the design phase. Let's just get to building, right?

My business partner and I often say that thinking is the hard part. The act of doing is pretty easy, once you know what you're doing and why. However, it is common practice to take action and plan at the same time. Or put another way, to build the plane while it is in the air. Over time, my business partner, Eric Page, adapted something he calls the "six-step process to get what you want out of life."

Try using the following six steps the next time you have a project or initiative that you're working on. By thinking through the problems before jumping to the solution too quickly, you will be more effective and targeted.

Exercise: The Six-Step Process to Get What You Want out of Life

This exercise lays out the steps to building a plan. Notice how the solution doesn't appear until step 4. The work is about getting clear on your goals, as well as the problems and the root causes that keep you (or your team) from achieving them.

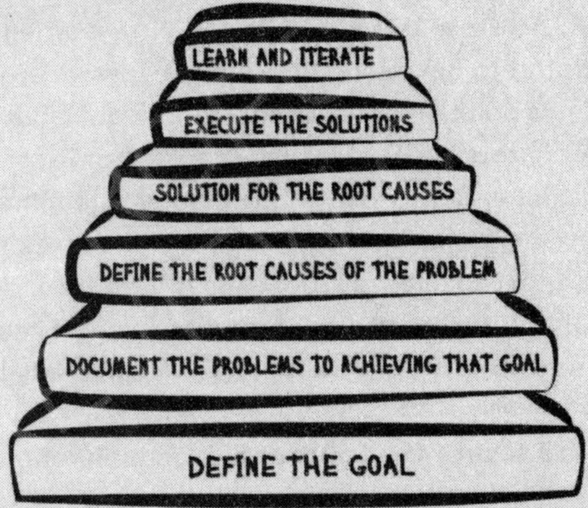

Step 1: Define the Goal. What is the problem that you are trying to solve? Sounds easy enough, but it becomes significantly more complicated when you are working with a group of people. It is incredible how often a group starts running off and doing stuff before there is clear agreement on the goal. Your time is valuable, so don't waste it on activities that aren't intentional.

Step 2: Document the Problems in the Way of Achieving That Goal. Brainstorm all the obstacles or reasons why your goal won't be achieved. Get them out there. Don't overthink it. If you're working with others, do this together. There is simply no greater relief than listing all the reasons why something won't work out.

Step 3: Define the Root Causes of the Problem. The problems you listed in step 2 all exist for a reason. Why is that the case? Why are they problems in the first place? Ask *why* for the problems you identified in step 2 and list the root causes.

Step 4: Address the Root Causes. Now is when things start to get interesting. Notice how we are building a solution not explicitly for the goal, but to attack the root causes that will keep us from achieving it. It is a lot easier to take action on a problem that is a component of achieving that goal than to tackle the whole enchilada. Not all root causes have the same level of priority or intensity. Prioritize the root causes that are the most significant blockers to success.

Step 5: Execute the Solutions. Execution represents the set of actions you (or others) will undertake to attack the root causes keeping you from achieving your goal. By definition, if you overcome the root causes, you will achieve your goal.

Step 6: Learn and Iterate. Once you have taken action, you are going to get some feedback on how effective you were. What did you learn? How does that learning inform the next step you are going to take? What did you learn about yourself? How would you go about it differently next time, if at all?

"Failure to plan is planning to fail."
–Russell Benaroya

I was definitely nervous. We had raised significant financing from a strategic investor for my last start-up in digital health, but the market wasn't responding as well as we would have liked. The anxiety-provoking thing about raising money from investors is that it starts a clock ticking. I had a small window to validate that we had a business that could find a foothold in the market and grow. I'd thought our hypothesis going into the business was sound, but it wasn't working out as I had expected.

I was in a meeting at my investor's office to talk about the market and ways to modify the business that could meet the market need and begin to show traction. The idea was to shift the business toward the employer market with a wellness solution that we could essentially give away for free. I loved the idea. I got a lot of energy from it. We decided to go all in and pursue it.

My desire for action to shift away from the thing that wasn't working to something that might work trumped the real need, which was to take a bit more time to plan and think through the implications of such a major shift. We would need to hire more people, divert our developer resources, and reimagine many facets of the product. But I was emboldened by a new path forward. I knew it would work. It had to work.

After six months and over a million dollars of investment later, we were ready to bring the product to market. Within the first month of launch, I knew we had missed a critical part of the process. I might have been energized and excited, but the market wasn't demanding it. I had mistaken action with creating value and let my fear of stillness get in the way. Rather than taking thirty days to think it through, document a plan, and conduct low-cost customer development that would either validate or invalidate the idea, I barreled headfirst into it. I'm a pretty convincing guy–to myself and those around me. So we went for it. The results were predictable, and the lesson was costly.

ACTION IS CREATING A WIN-4-ALL

We waste so much energy when we aren't in sync with those around us, and taking action usually involves or impacts someone else in your life (friends, family, and colleagues). Action might be an investment we make, a project that we launch, a new hire, or a creative partnership. It is rare that action is an entirely solitary endeavor. Action that is out of sync with others usually comes from convincing ourselves that we are right and that someone else is wrong. Once we convince them we are right, everything will resolve itself. But does it? Absolutely not. In fact, it more often creates an even greater rift. The idea of seeking a Win-4-All is not about making sure everyone around you is in agreement. Rather, it is about an openness and a curiosity to understand how someone perceives (their story) the impact of your action. To achieve a Win-4-All requires:

1. **Listening deeply to understand the interests, needs, and goals of the other person or party.** We are so ready to advance our own agenda that we're just waiting to start talking again. The harder we push to make the other person understand us, the more likely they are to see our point of view, right? Wrong. It is the other way around. Listen and be curious until the other person is fully heard. And then ask, "Is there more?"
2. **Reflecting back to confirm understanding.** Our internal operating system hears things in a way that makes sense to us, so reflecting back what we heard helps confirm that we fully understood what the other person meant. The best way to affirm that is by repeating what we think we heard and then asking, "Is that right?" If they say, "Yes, that's right," then you can move on.
3. **Expressing your desires.** Listening deeply isn't about subordinating your desires in favor of making others around you happy. As a coach of mine once said, "If you're not at the table for a Win-4-All, it's not a Win-4-All." You must be seen and heard, and that is what you are going

to ask for: "I want you to see me and understand me. Can you do that?"

4. **Creating choices.** We all desire some form of control, and when we take that away from people, they often feel cornered or manipulated. An effective Win-4-All strategy is to create choices where you are indifferent to the outcome.

Achieving a Win-4-All will significantly reduce friction in taking action around your life design. A Win-4-All is not about making everyone happy, especially not at the expense of your life design. A Win-4-All is about having empathy and being aware that the wake that you create in pursuit of your life design will impact people you care about, or the people you want to be your allies, in many different ways. Seeing and hearing them and helping them see and hear you will create a smoother path.

"Make empathy your superpower."
–Sarah Dusek, cofounder and former CEO, Under Canvas

We were successful building and growing Under Canvas because of the relationships that we built with landowners. Anyone who's ever bought rural land will know that landowners can be a cantankerous bunch! But the key for us was understanding their interests and needs and where they intersected with what we were trying to accomplish.

It's not that you always need to like the people, but you need to know what motivates them. We would partner with landowners near national parks to set up Under Canvas on their properties. Some were very difficult, aggressive, and old school.

I had one landowner that we did a deal with that had a large number of charred trees on his property. He was absolutely passionate/crazy/obsessed with these trees and insisted that no development could happen on the site that would touch one of these dead trees. It was vitally important for me to connect with his concern and share our intent as a company and our mission and how we would treat and develop land. I finally managed to convince him that we were not going to touch the trees. I was willing to put into the contract that I would not harm the dead trees in order to demonstrate I cared about what he cared about.

Getting deals done means you have to understand what's important to somebody else. There is often more going on than just money. There's sentiment. There's history. There are memories. There's *So-and-so's girlfriend's daughter's mother tripped over this stone over here, and we built a memorial to her.* There is always all sorts of stuff going on in a deal, and unless you can be empathetic to how somebody feels, it's harder to get them to the table and harder to get them to transact with you.

I think in small-town America, outside of corporate-world transactions, deals are not all about money. The same usual drivers don't apply. Understanding that is a key to unlocking new opportunities and creating growth in unexpected ways. Empathy is a key to making things happen.

ACTION IS FOCUSING ON YOUR CURRENT GAME

In 2016, I was the CEO of EveryMove, a digital health company funded by a notable group of strategic investors. The previous five years had been a wild ride. We had made some inroads with our software but hadn't found a sustainable product market fit. In other words, we were still trying to figure out where we delivered measurable value for our customer. My cofounder and I had separated, the market was shifting, and we were going to need to adapt to stay relevant. I was frustrated because the investors were our ideal customers, but I repeatedly ran into a brick wall when trying to secure commercial agreements with them. I felt trapped and frustrated and had to admit I was unlikely to succeed. I felt myself wanting to jump to the next opportunity as the situation became increasingly uncomfortable. I didn't want to be lost at sea when the ship went down. Oh, and it was very convenient for me to blame others for the circumstances rather than take responsibility.

But in that year, I had a conversation with a mentor who shared his approach to playing the game. He said, "Russell, do you think when Russell Wilson [the Seattle Seahawks quarterback] is in the game with two minutes to go and his team is down, he says, 'Hey, guys, it looks like we're going to lose. Let's start thinking about next week'? No. He doesn't. Russell Wilson gets into the huddle and, with the best information that he has, makes the best call that he can to keep moving the ball down the field. He may get to the end zone. That might still not win the game. The point is that great athletes play until the last second of the game they are in. And only when they have finished that game do they learn from it and start looking ahead to the next week. There is always going to be a next game, so finish the one that you are in as strongly and with as much integrity as you can. Then, focus on what's next."

It was the right advice at the right time. We were able to effectively sell the company four months later as we focused intently on finishing the game.

It is so easy to want to escape an uncomfortable situation by hopping onto the next job, project, or relationship, because that will bring you relief. And it does, for a while, but you will fall right back into the same pattern over and over again. When you take action, focus it on the current game. Put your energy into finishing it well. The power of your focus will yield not only a much better outcome but also significantly more learning for future decisions.

"To stay in the game, you have to have endurance."

–James Mayo, cofounder and CEO, SOS Hydrate

I was a pro runner, and I am a former Army officer. Dehydration was a major issue, and I suffered from it firsthand. My brother was also a pro runner, and he actually collapsed from dehydration at the World

Championship in South Africa. My wife was a physician in Mexico treating patients with oral hydration therapy and IV drips. The solution on the market for major dehydration was oral rehydration solution, but that was administered to patients who were vomiting and had diarrhea. We wanted to create something that was more commercial, to treat dehydration in athletes. Like many things, this idea popped up over a few glasses of wine. We came up with the name, SOS Hydrate, and I decided to leave my job and go for it.

As a former pro athlete, I understand the grit that is required to stay in the game to finish the race, and this one at SOS Hydrate has been more like an ultramarathon. We came into this industry without beverage experience. We didn't know the rules of the game, and, in some ways, that has been a good thing, because we had to chart our own course and not just do what every other beverage company has to put up with. We didn't have the funds to launch a ready-to-drink solution, so we developed the powder packets. My coach always said, "Run your own race," and I have to keep reminding myself of that. When I see that companies that I believe have a far less compelling offering are raising significant capital, it can throw me off.

My response is to get out there and make more sales, meet more people, and create more connections. My strategy has been to hire athletes because they are hard and gritty, know how to run a race, and know they will lose more often than they will win. And a lot of the training of the team has been around tenacity, because to stay in this game, you have to have endurance. And we do.

AND FINALLY, ACTION IS PATIENCE

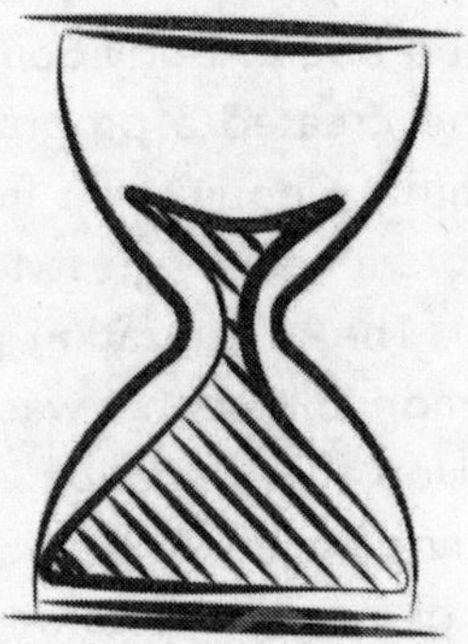

It feels appropriate that we shift in this chapter from talking about action as disruptive to talking about action as being about patience. Don't confuse patience with complacence. Action does not mean you are in constant motion; it means that you are observant of where you are in relation to the individuals and environment around you. How are people reacting to you and your principles? What is happening inside your organization where you are realizing energy gains or energy drains? How are your friends or family creating unnecessary drama and trying to pull you into it? How can you avoid taking the bait? There is often an instinct to want to get into the mix and take control because you seek rapid resolution. Try a different approach. Try to be patient.

"It's OK to hang around the watercooler."
–Russell Benaroya

In the early 2000s, I was on the board of a nonprofit in Los Angeles called Sound Body Sound Mind. Sound Body Sound Mind created a program that installed state-of-the-art fitness equipment in inner city high schools to promote a healthy lifestyle for all kids (not just the athletes). The organization was founded by Bill and Cindy Simon. Bill's father was secretary of the treasury in the Nixon administration, and Bill ran a private investment firm called William E. Simon & Sons. Bill was the type of mentor who always made me feel important. He took the time to learn about me and was always available. He could tell I was antsy in my current role working for a private equity group in Los Angeles. He could tell that I wanted to make a move.

One day, he said something to me that I dismissed at the time but have come to realize is profoundly true. He said, "Russell, you know that sometimes it's OK to hang around the watercooler for a little bit and see how things progress. You might be surprised what opportunities can arrive when you're patient and observing. Action is not always about movement. It is about being alert and aware." What? Hanging out is a form of action? Bah. I was sure Bill didn't know what he was talking about.

Oh, but Bill absolutely knew what he was talking about. I just wasn't listening. And what probably felt to Bill like an off-the-cuff comment stuck with me. Now, I reflect on how little I took that advice for many years.

Bill was anything but complacent. What I took away from him was that if I could slow down a bit and observe my environment and be a bit more intentional, opportunities would present themselves. Don't try to control the universe. Let it unfold and be ready to say yes when the right opportunity arises. And be happy saying no if you aren't convinced that the action in front of you is worth taking. I was so anxious to be doing the next great thing that I never fully finished the game that I was playing. Over the years, I created a lot of really interesting experiences—but without particular intention around the life I was creating.

After twenty years, I still remember this conversation with Bill because it was so counter to what I had always assumed action to be. Since the advice was coming from a guy who had navigated high-stakes deals and transactions, his comments rocked me even more. Action is production, I thought. Action is being in a state of motion. Wrong. Action is about developing a keen sense of awareness of your surroundings and how you navigate them. Just because you are not actively in motion doesn't mean you aren't taking action.

TAKE ACTION
CHAPTER SUMMARY

What we learned in this chapter is that you can lay out your life design foundation, but if you are not willing to act, you won't shift. We also learned that action is more than just moving. Action is about learning. Here are the highlights.

- Action is not about a predetermined outcome. You move with intention, not because you know how things are going to turn out.
- Action is disruptive. It is not intended to make everyone happy. It is intended to put you on a course of your design.
- Fear is part of us and isn't to be repelled. Accept it as part of the process of taking action.
- Most of us break down when it comes to action because we don't have a plan. Planning is essential to figuring out where to put your energy.
- Action does not mean that you win and everyone else loses. You can achieve your goal and help those around you achieve theirs as well. Creating a Win-4-All takes curiosity and an openness to hearing other points of view.
- You can only play one game at a time. Focus on it and finish it.
- Patience is a core component of action. Watching and observing are part of the process.

TAKE ACTION
CHAPTER SUMMARY

The Exercise in This Chapter

- The Six-Step Process to Get What You Want out of Life

Highlighted Designers

- "Everyone told me I was crazy. Like, nuts."
  —Lori Torres
- "I made fear my ally."
  —Max Nelson
- "Optimism is not a plan."
  —David Nilssen
- "Failure to plan is planning to fail."
  —Russell Benaroya
- "Make empathy your superpower."
  —Sarah Dusek
- "To stay in the game, you have to have endurance."
  —James Mayo
- "It's OK to hang around the watercooler."
  —Russell Benaroya

ONE LIFE TO LEAD—INTEGRATING LIFE DESIGN INTO BUSINESS SUCCESS

"Don't make decisions based on fear: fear of failure or fear of losing money or reputation. It's natural to fear coming up short, but I make a conscientious effort to value more the 'going for it' and accept the risk of potentially coming up short. And when I have come up short, I've chosen to see it as a practice run for me to learn, adjust, and then take another run at it. Success isn't always in one shot. Sometimes it is, but I think more often it's refining, retargeting, and trying again."

–Madeline Haydon, founder and CEO, nutpods

Notice what is happening inside of you as you think about what it would feel like to be free to design the life you desire. Notice what it feels like to be in alignment in how you live and how you lead. Notice how you feel more equipped to lead in your business because you feel more control to lead in your life. Are you dismissing it as unattainable? Does it make you nervous? Are you wondering where you would even begin?

Have you ever considered that you have allowed the circumstances of your life to drive your plan, rather than the other way around? Shifting toward your life design shows a willingness to view the world around you from the perspective of abundance, not limitation. The steps to start making moves can happen for you today.

Begin with taking a breath before you charge into your day, take on that next project, connect with a group of people, or perform your obligatory duties. Check yourself. Run your life design diagnostic:

1. Do I have a story about this that drains my energy?
2. Am I living in accordance with my principles?
3. Is this an environment where I get energy?
4. Am I in my genius zone?
5. Am I taking action to support my life design?

IT'S YOUR TIME: SMALL CHANGES CREATE BIG IMPACTS

Simply put, adopting the mind-set that you are in control of your life design is a game changer. Wake up in the morning and say, "I am in control. The decisions that I make today are mine." Small changes will have a big impact. Here are some small change ideas to practice on a weekly basis.

Exercise: Small Shifts

WEEK OF:

1. **I Found an Energy Spot:** Find one place where you feel open and creative and relaxed, and go there once a week. It could be in your home, or a café, or driving alone in your car. This week, here is where I found an energy spot and why it worked for me: ________________

2. **I Labeled a Story:** When you are getting a little worked up about a situation, notice whether it's a fact or a story. Label the story. Acknowledge that it's your story. It's not something that needs to be solved. The very act of stopping to see it is a win! Here is a story I told myself this week that did not serve me: ________________

3. **I Shared a Principle:** Share one or more of your principles with someone in your life. It's not necessarily for them, but it is for you to feel seen and heard. Put your principles out in the universe and watch how they come to life. Here is the principle that I shared this week with someone and why I did it: ________________

4. **I Got into my Genius Zone:** Do one thing this week that you can point to and say you were in your genius zone. Celebrate it. Capture that feeling in the moment. This week, I shifted to spend more time in my genius zone by doing the following: ________________

5. **I Took Action:** Commit to one small, courageous act. It could be a difficult conversation with a friend or loved one. It could be sharing your genius zone with your boss. It could be going on a walk midweek in the park and having a walking meeting because that is where you get energy. I took action this week on my life design by doing the following: ____________

If you are motivated to take control and design your life, then begin with small steps. They will compound in benefit and velocity. Your courage will build. You will see that those micro risks you took didn't have negative consequences—or if they did, they weren't catastrophic. In fact, it will probably be the opposite: succeeding at small challenges can help you feel lighter and more in control.

As you get comfortable with freeing yourself from the cage of your current circumstances or from lamenting about what you thought your life should be based on a fictional story you made up, you will make bigger design changes. The power that you create around yourself will be felt by those around you. People will be attracted to your energy because they see you as someone who knows what they want and where they are going. You will find that the environment around you will begin to conspire to support you, to lift you up, to open doors and pathways that you never thought were possible. And you will notice it. You might think it's crazy now, but it will happen.

HOW FACTS, PRINCIPLES, GENIUS ZONE, AND ENERGY INTERACT

Integration of the steps of life design is the magic of the idea of one life to lead. While you may work on these independently, it is integrating them into your life that fuels sustainable change.

> **Facts** are foundational and will help you identify and isolate the stories that may or may not be serving you.
>
> Your **Principles** represent the code of behavior in which you want to act.
>
> Your **Genius Zone** is where you are able to act on your unique capability.
>
> Your **Energy** is about finding the right environment, where you are inspired to be at your best.

You may be in your genius zone managing a team, but the work environment you are in is toxic, the customers you serve are painful, and you are holed up in some small cubicle day in and day out. That's not optimizing your life design. Sure, you may be in your genius zone, but your overall life design formula is out of balance. With these new tools and insights, you can now begin to dissect circumstances in your life where you feel stuck: *How am I contributing to my situation? Am I out of integrity with my principles? Am I in an environment that is draining my energy? Or am I simply not in my genius zone?*

What I want you to appreciate is that there is no blame here, not for you or for anyone else. *You* get to do the work and take the actions to make the changes you want. *You* are in control of your life design.

The following exercise will help you to look at certain activities in your life where you feel stuck, determine the root cause of the problem, and then prompt you to take action, focusing on the right life design principle.

Exercise: Getting Unstuck

Step 1: Set Up Your Chart

Create a sheet for yourself using the illustration below as an example.

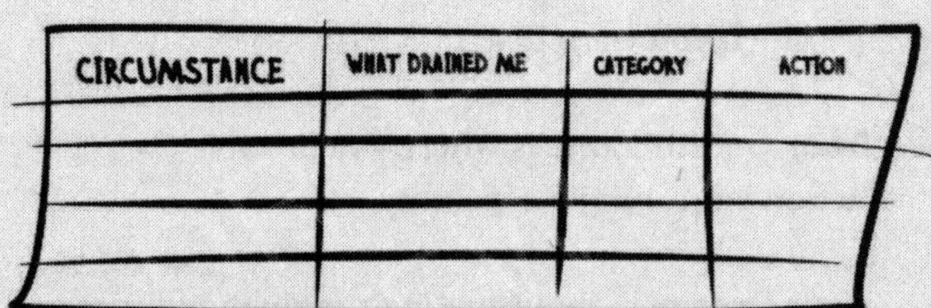

Step 2: Define the Circumstance

Think back over the last several weeks to activities that felt draining or laborious (circumstances). Even consider things that you didn't do or that you procrastinated on. It could have been a project you were working on, a meeting you were in, or an individual you were interacting with. It may be subtle, so don't rush this. The feeling could have been fleeting, but you know that something was off. Write these down on your sheet in the column labeled "Circumstance."

Hint: Consider taking a look at your calendar if you are looking for something to jog your memory. (Heck, I barely remember what I ate for breakfast.)

Step 3: Assess

For each of these activities, ask yourself what drained you. Don't try to employ any technical jargon, just let it flow. Some responses might be:

- I love this work but don't enjoy the person I'm working with.
- The problem to solve is exciting. The process to get there with the team is soul sucking.
- The work isn't complicated, it's just that I'm not being used at my highest level. Someone else could do that.
- I am being asked to do something that goes against my principles.

Step 4: Categorize

For each of those activities, categorize them as compromising one or more of your:

- Principles (living in accordance with my code).
- Energy (the environment that fuels my sense of freedom).
- Genius Zone (what I can uniquely do and that feels effortless).

This is a really important section, because it will set the stage for how you take action to reduce these drains in your life.

Step 5: Allocate
Now look at each of these items and where you compromised your life design in terms of your genius zone, energy, or principles. The options available to you are to (i) delegate items away, (ii) improve or change the process and systems, or (iii) confront the threat to your principles.

Delegate: For those items that aren't in your genius zone, delegate them away. Who else could do this work either equally well or better than you? I find that this applies to many administrative tasks in the workplace and with tasks around the house. How can you outsource this or work with your team to redefine your areas of responsibility? One of the great things about the freelance economy is the ability to delegate certain tasks. I thank my lucky stars every day for Upwork and Fiverr, two freelance marketplaces that will help you with a myriad of tasks. If you feel stuck in a current role that is just not in your genius zone, your life design commitment is to either redefine your role in your current organization or create a plan to move.

Improve the Process: For those items that compromised your energy, look at modifying the process of how they are getting done. Is there an easier way to do it? Could you automate it? Is there a better system to put in place? Examples of this could be a better process for how meetings are conducted, or the frequency of certain meetings. It could be that the spreadsheet you keep on updating because that's how it has always been done needs a full overhaul. Step back and look at how you might change the process to significantly improve your energy level.

Confront the Threat: For those areas that risk compromising or actually do compromise your principles, your decision is one of integrity. Remember, when you compromise your principles, you are out of integrity with what you believe and how you are acting. So principles really become a nonnegotiable for you. It seems so black-and-white, but it's amazing how complicated it can become. Why? Because we have brains and those brains are pretty good at rationalizing why it's OK, just this one time, to compromise. You know it when those moments come up. There is this feeling in your gut that is just a little bit unsettled. You can live with it, but it eats at you. It's always there. When you're clear and have identified it, here are your options:

1. **Share your feelings around this situation.** When you do this without blame or judgment, it tends to be a lot easier. "I feel bad (or sad, angry, frustrated, etc.) because I am doing XYZ, and I'm out of integrity with my principles." Remember, this isn't about what is being done to you but about the situation you have found yourself in.

2. **Second, change the situation.** Take control of your circumstance. No one is making you do anything. Leave. Find an environment that is more in line with how you want to live your life. It's not easy, but neither is living in a persistent state of compromise.

IT TOOK A WHILE TO GET HERE–GO EASY ON YOURSELF

When I returned from Costa Rica I thought I had solved it. I thought that I had overcome the challenges that had made me a victim to circumstance. And to a large degree, I had. I worried a whole lot less about what other people thought about me. I didn't feel the need to plug back into my old social and business network. I realized that no one really cared that much about what I did or didn't do. I could focus on the life I wanted to live with the people I wanted to live it with. My whole mentality was not that I was "returning" to Seattle, but that I was moving to Seattle. A new city. A new lens. A new adventure. But it's never that simple.

As I settled back into the norms of the day to day, reacquainting myself with my comfortable surroundings, getting back into the flow of information, where I could see what other people were doing with their lives, I felt jealousy and restlessness creeping back in. The difference was that this time, I didn't let it bother me—I accepted it. I know that designing my life does not mean that I am immune to the forces around me. It means that I can observe how I am feeling, acknowledge it, and move on.

I am more grounded in my principles, and I don't let stories that are not in service to my life invade my space for too long. But it is going to happen to me, and it's going to happen to you, too. There is a force that wants to pull you back into the machine of how you are "supposed" to be or what you "should" do. The work in front of you is to go easy on yourself. Stay supported by your pillars of life design:

- Ground your stories with facts.

- Establish your principles.
- Harness the energy.
- Get in and stay in your genius zone.
- Take action.

ONE LIFE TO LEAD

You have the design tools to create the life you want. It is within your power to design now. It is within you to be a stronger leader because you prioritize your life design and show up in a way that is your authentic self. You can start today. You are ready, or you wouldn't have read to this last section of the book. You have made the commitment. Tell the people around you that you're ready to shift and begin.

All of the Designers whose stories you read had to grapple with and continue to wrangle their life designs to become the type of business leaders that will make the kind of impact they intend to. Throw in a little bit of luck—because remember, you are a lucky person—and great things can happen. We are all a work in progress and lucky to be able to make meaningful changes when we are equipped with the knowledge of how to do it.

You are ready to do it. You are ready for a better life design.

INDEX OF DESIGNER STORIES

Step 3: Harness Energy from the Environment

Step 4: Get in and Stay in Your Genius Zone

- "I am the storyteller."
  —Madeline Haydon
- "Eventually, he fired me."
  —Sharelle Klaus

Step 5: Take Action

- "Everyone told me I was crazy. Like, nuts."
  —Lori Torres
- "I made fear my ally."
  —Max Nelson
- "Optimism is not a plan."
  —David Nilssen
- "Failure to plan is planning to fail."
  —Russell Benaroya
- "Make empathy your superpower."
  —Sarah Dusek
- "To stay in the game, you have to have endurance."
  —James Mayo
- "It's OK to hang around the watercooler."
  —Russell Benaroya

INDEX OF EXERCISES

Integrating Life Design into Business Success

DESIGNER PROFESSIONAL BIOS

If you want to read the business backgrounds of these folks, go ahead. It's always interesting to read lists of people's accomplishments, but recognize that this is largely a veneer. Underneath every accolade and milestone is someone doing the work to figure out how to design their life.

SARAH DUSEK
COFOUNDER AND FORMER CEO, UNDER CANVAS

I am the cofounder and former CEO at Under Canvas, Inc. My husband, Jacob, and I were so inspired by the African safari experience that we set out to create an immersive outdoor escape that serves as a unique bridge between travel and the outdoors. We started Under Canvas in 2009 with the opening of an all-inclusive glamping adventure resort and have grown it to include nine luxury glamping resorts and customized event offerings, bringing the glamping experience to life anywhere in the country. I am proud that we have been recognized as the "perfect glamping experience" by *Vogue*. We operate locations in Yellowstone and Glacier in Montana; Moab and Zion in Utah; Mount Rushmore in South Dakota; Great Smoky Mountains in Tennessee; and Grand Canyon and Lake Powell, Arizona; and in Acadia, Maine.

FRAN DUNAWAY
COFOUNDER AND CEO, TOMBOYX

I am a media executive-turned-fashion entrepreneur and cofounder of TomboyX, a Seattle-based gender-neutral underwear and loungewear brand launched in 2013. The brand started as a passion project in collaboration with my wife and cofounder, Naomi Gonzalez, to create the perfect button-up shirt, pivoting to focus on underwear based on the overwhelming demand for the first boxer brief for women. As CEO, I have led TomboyX to double yearly growth and am honored to have received industry recognition including a listing on *Inc.* magazine's five hundred fastest-growing companies and being named Small Business of the Year for King County and Fastest-Growing Minority-Owned Company by the *Puget Sound Business Journal*. I am active in social causes and serve as executive director of Equal Rights Washington, a nonprofit focused on LGBTQ rights that successfully advocated for passage of antidiscrimination legislation (Washington House Bill 2661) in 2006. I also served on the steering committee and board of governors of the Human Rights Campaign's Seattle chapter.

NICK SOMAN
FOUNDER AND CEO, DECENT

I am the founder and CEO of Decent, a company that is bringing affordable health care to the small business market. I started my career in 2004 as a senior consultant at Strategic Decisions Group. In 2010–2011, I was a senior product manager for Amazon Kindle. In 2011, I became the founder and CEO of Reveal Chat, a chat app. In 2015–2016, I served as a new product owner at Napster. Later, I worked also as a growth product lead at Gusto and growth mentor at Reforge.

MAX NELSON
FOUNDER AND CEO, HOOD

I am the founder of HOOD, a premium line of customized ball caps made from high-quality merino wool. I call it the Steve Jobs approach to making a hat, where no detail, inside or out, has been missed. HOOD sits at the intersection of community, personality, and fashion. Hats can be customized with the logo of the neighborhood that you live in, and they make a statement. When I created the first hat two years ago, people started asking where they could get one. And, well . . . an idea was born. Before HOOD, I was a real estate broker for many years in Southern California.

MATT OPPENHEIMER
COFOUNDER AND CEO, REMITLY

I am the cofounder and CEO of Remitly, the mobile-first provider of remittances and financial services for immigrants, customers who transfer billions of dollars annually. Remitly's vision is to transform the lives of millions of immigrants and their families with the most trusted financial services products on the planet. Founded initially to disrupt the nearly $600 billion global remittance industry, Remitly uses a reliable and convenient mobile app that eliminates the long wait times, complexities, and fees typical of traditional remittance processes, returning millions of dollars in savings and spending power to immigrants every year. I began working on the problem immediately as an entrepreneur in residence at Highway 12 Ventures in Idaho and launched the company from TechStars in Seattle. I was proud to be named EY Entrepreneur of the Year 2016 in the Pacific Northwest and to be recognized as a *Puget Sound Business Journal* 40 Under 40 honoree for my work with

Remitly. I have an MBA from Harvard Business School and a bachelor's degree in psychology from Dartmouth College.

MADELINE HAYDON
FOUNDER AND CEO, NUTPODS

I am the founder of nutpods, a dairy-free, plant-based creamer alternative to half-and-half. I wanted a creamer that tasted good without a lot of sugar and processed ingredients. Nutpods has achieved incredible success in the face of much larger consumer packaged goods companies. What makes nutpods such an incredible and unlikely story is that I had no experience in the industry. I worked in a nonprofit before this, but we started a movement through a highly successful Kickstarter campaign in 2013. I am proud that we have revolutionized the sleepy category of processed creamers and also put nutpods on the international stage (#2 in the five thousand fastest-growing food and beverage companies in *Inc.* magazine). In 2019, I was honored as an Ernst & Young Entrepreneur of the Year in the Pacific Northwest and also received the Amazon Small Business of the Year award.

KIRBY WINFIELD
GENERAL PARTNER, ASCEND VC

I am a start-up operator and investor and currently the founding general partner at Ascend VC, a preseed-stage venture fund investing in marketplace, e-commerce/DTC, and B2B software start-ups in the Pacific Northwest. Early in my career, I was a founding team member and operating executive at tech start-ups Go2Net (GNET) and Marchex (MCHX). I was also a two-time venture capital–backed CEO with AdXpose (DFJ, Ignition), acquired by comScore (SCOR), and Dwellable (Maveron, VersionOne), acquired by HomeAway (AWAY).

I currently serve as a board director at Bean Box, the premier direct-to-consumer gourmet coffee gift and subscription brand; Keepe, the leading vetted, on-demand contractor network for property managers; and SyncFloor, the consumer-grade music licensing platform for independent labels and artists. I have served as board chair at Special Olympics of Washington, where I helped bring the 2018 Special Olympics USA Games to Seattle. I am a member of the board of trustees of Seattle Preparatory School, a board member at the University of Washington's Haring Center Capital Campaign, and a board advisor at the Friendship Circle of Washington.

LORI TORRES
FOUNDER AND CEO, PARCEL PENDING

I am the founder and CEO of Parcel Pending, the leading provider of package management solutions for residential, commercial, retail, and university properties in the United States and Canada. I launched Parcel Pending after working in property management for over twenty-five years. I am honored to have been named an EY Entrepreneur of the Year 2019 Orange County and 2017 Innovator of the Year by the *Orange County Business Journal* and to have been chosen as one of thirteen entrepreneurs admitted into the EY Entrepreneurial Winning Women 2017, North America class. Parcel Pending sold to Neopost in December 2019 for $100 million.

DAVID NILSSEN
COFOUNDER AND CEO, GUIDANT FINANCIAL

I am the cofounder of Guidant Financial. Since launching in 2003, Guidant Financial has become a leader in small business financing and self-directed IRAs. In 2007, I was named the Small Business Administration's (SBA) National Young

Entrepreneur of the Year. I was also named a two-time finalist for an Ernst & Young Entrepreneur of the Year award. Guidant has helped nearly twenty thousand entrepreneurial-minded individuals access $4.5 billion to start or acquire a small business or franchise. I am also the author of *Making the Jump into Small Business Ownership.*

SHARELLE KLAUS
FOUNDER AND CEO, DRY SODA COMPANY

I founded DRY Soda Company, the leading lightly carbonated beverage for celebrating any occasion. I was an early entrant into the sparkling beverage industry and one of the first female founders in a heavily male-dominated industry. After having four children, I didn't want to let a lack of wine or cocktails stop me from creating a great pairing. I am an avid supporter of entrepreneurship and frequently speak at professional conferences, workshops, and the University of Washington Business School. I have served as a member of the executive committee of the Seattle Pacific University Business School, the board of directors of the Seattle Chamber of Commerce, and the board of the Seattle Lung Force. I currently serve on the board of directors of Aliados, an Ecuador-based foundation that works to build resilient community businesses based on biodiversity in the Andes and the Amazon. I graduated from Seattle Pacific University with an undergraduate degree in political science and currently reside in Seattle, where I live with my four children and my German shepherd, Lennox.

JAMES MAYO
COFOUNDER AND CEO, SOS HYDRATE

I am the cofounder and CEO of SOS Hydrate. SOS is a fast-acting electrolyte replacement as effective as an IV drip and the world's fastest-absorbing hydration mix for athletes. I founded the company with my brother and my wife, who is a physician in Arizona. I didn't have any beverage experience before starting SOS, but I'm proud today that SOS is recognized for its impact around the world. Prior to SOS, I was an officer in the Army for six years. I also ran for my country, Britain, and was the national mile champion.

CASEY ROLOFF
FOUNDER AND CEO, SEABROOK

I created a town called Seabrook on the Washington coast. What started out with thirty-four acres of raw land is today a model of New Urbanism, a walkable community that sits atop a bluff overlooking the Pacific Ocean. Today we have built over four hundred houses there, have seventeen parks, a town hall, and community retail locations. What I really care about is creating better communities where people can live. I wasn't a great student, and I didn't grow up with a bunch of money around me. I just had this drive, a tenacity to pursue my goals. I am committed to working in concert with the environment and to supporting the community. The future of town-building is about creating places where people get energy to be their best selves.

ACKNOWLEDGMENTS

I never thought I would write a book, and certainly not this book. For many years, I was so disconnected from my true feelings that everything felt inauthentic. But, slowly, the barriers began to come down as I rebuilt a foundation based on my principles. There are lots of designers who influenced my approach as an entrepreneur, a father, a runner, a husband, and a friend.

Of course this book would not have much impact if it weren't for the generous contribution of the "Designers" in *One Life to Lead*. Thank you, Matt, Fran, Madeline, Sarah, Lori, Nick, Casey, Max, David, Kirby, Sharelle, and James.

I really have to thank the Seattle Entrepreneurs' Organization for putting the mirror up to me early. My original forum members were Andy Liu, Matt Watson, Alissa Leinonen, Bob Thordarson, Mark Whitmore, Raja Mukerji, Kristin Knight, Boaz Ashkenazy, and Marc Rousso.

When Al Osborne from the UCLA Anderson School of Management agreed to write the foreword for the book, I was elated. Al is an iconic figure in entrepreneurship and leadership and has helped plant the seeds of possibility for thousands of individuals. Thank you, Al, for making the time to support the growth of one. If I have done one thing right, that is having some exceptional business coaches. Lex Sisney and Phil Dembo not only helped change my vocabulary but reoriented me to the type of person I wanted to become, even if I was not quite ready to go there. Your inspiration is woven throughout this book.

I want to thank my business partner, Eric Page, who has traversed the course of two and a half start-ups with me. No one thought we would make it together, but we have grown on each other like any good rash. I have learned so much from you about being relentless in curiosity and seeking truth. I appreciate so much you introducing me to the Conscious Leadership Group and the multiple ways that it has impacted my life.

One Life to Lead would not be complete without acknowledging my parents, who have always been there to support me even if some of my experiments raised an eyebrow or two.

Y es importante reconocer a mis amigos en Costa Rica, José Gutiérrez y Cristián Roberts. Me recibieron con los brazos abiertos y me dieron la oportunidad de explorar nuevas posibilidades.

I am indebted to the trails in the Cascade Mountains in Washington that have been my playground for physical and mental health over the last decade. You have treated me well and given me the courage to take on big challenges.

I want to give a special shout-out to Girl Friday Productions who held my hand through this process and gracefully (and patiently) navigated me to this finished product. And to Marni Seneker, who provided me with the developmental editing for *One Life to Lead*. I called on you because I knew you would give it to me straight. And you did. I also want to thank Tamta Kondzharia for the fantastic freehand images throughout the book.

I want to acknowledge my children, Devon and Shane. I knew I would learn a lot from you but couldn't have imagined how profoundly you would teach me about myself.

And most of all, I want to thank my wife, Melissa. Through all my self-righteousness, you stuck with me. Through all my start-ups, you gave me a lot of rope. And when I was ready to stop fighting to be what I thought other people wanted, you were ready to take the journey with me, as a partner. We built a fence around our relationship and have held it sacred. For that, I am grateful.

NOTES

In this section I have included a list of references, notes, and citations. I am sure that there is someone that I have failed to give credit to in this book. If I've ascribed an idea of yours to someone else or failed to recognize your contributions, please let me know by emailing me at russell@benaroya.net. That said, my attempt here is to give as much credit as possible to the people and sources I relied on.

GET INTO THE DESIGN MIND-SET

When people wrote down their goals, they were 33 percent more likely to achieve them: Matthews, G. (2015). Goal Research Summary. Paper presented at the 9th Annual International Conference of the Psychology Research Unit of Athens Institute for Education and Research (ATINER), Athens, Greece.

Dweck's work demonstrates the value of thinking in terms of experiments: Dweck, Carol S. *Mindset: The New Psychology of Success* (New York: Random House, 2006).

Goals tend to be very binary (you either did it or you failed) and can have unintended consequences if you're

not successful. Lisa D. Ordóñez et al. "Goals Gone Wild: The Systematic Side Effects of Over-Prescribing Goal Setting," *Academy of Management Perspectives*, Vol. 23, No. 1., 2009.

Gay Hendricks and Carol Kline in *Conscious Luck* offer a simple but profound message: by simply identifying ourselves as lucky and making the conscious decision to be a lucky person, we will create circumstances in our lives that seem lucky. Hendricks, Gay, and Carol Kline. *Conscious Luck* (New York: St. Martin's Essentials, 2020).

STEP 1: GROUND STORIES WITH FACTS

It is our ability to create and believe fiction that has kept us alive. Harari, Yuval Noah. *Sapiens: A Brief History of Humankind* (New York: Harper, 2015).

The most dangerous stories we tell ourselves are usually about our worthiness. Brown, Brené, *Rising Strong* (New York: Spiegel and Grau, 2015). You can also check out Brené's famous TED Talk: Brown, B. (2010, June). *The Power of Vulnerability* [Video]. TED Conferences. https://www.ted.com/talks/brene_brown_the_power_of_vulnerability?language=en.

One of my coaches, Lex Sisney, shared a concept with me called belief bubbles. I credit Lex Sisney with this term for how you are in control of creating your stories. He shared a presentation I gave in 2014 on his blog where I referenced belief bubbles specifically: "Want to Dent the Future? You Should Probably Get a Coach," https://organizationalphysics.com/2014/04/01/want-to-dent-the-future-you-should-probably-get-a-coach/, April 2104.

"Wow, Russell, this sounds like a 'get to.'" Huge props to my friend and mentor Andy Sack, who imparted this wisdom to me during a time when I thought I was screwed.

STEP 2: ESTABLISH YOUR PRINCIPLES

The most well-known architect of principles is Ray Dalio, the famous hedge fund manager who wrote a book conveniently titled *Principles*. Dalio, Ray. *Principles: Life and Work* (New York, Simon and Schuster, 2017).

Everything he does is driven by how he believes communities should be built, such as maximizing connection to each other and the environment, in a movement called New Urbanism. New Urbanism is not a term that Casey Roloff coined. It is an understood approach for planning and development. You can learn more about it at https://www.cnu.org/resources/what-new-urbanism.

STEP 3: HARNESS ENERGY FROM THE ENVIRONMENT

I learned about the concept of energy in my life from Lex Sisney, my friend and coach and the author of *Organizational Physics*. Sisney, Lex. *Organizational Physics* (Lulu.com, 2013). Check out Lex's blog at www.organizationalphysics.com.

By coincidence, sitting on our coffee table was the November 2017 issue of *National Geographic*, highlighting the happiest places on Earth. On the cover? Costa

Rica. Buettner, Dan. "The Search for Happiness." *National Geographic*, November 2017. Costa Rica's happiness recipe is a combination of enjoying the moment, family bonding, universal health, education, peace, faith, equality, and generosity.

Seek Approval from Within. I want to acknowledge the enormous impact that the book *The 15 Commitments of Conscious Leadership* (Jim Dethmer, Diana Chapman, and Kaley Klemp, 2015) has had on my life. The authors share that we all strive for three needs: control, security, and approval. When we can source those needs internally, we are free. It is in the pursuit of those from outside of ourselves where we get twisted up.

As my coach Phil used to say, "Live your worth. Don't prove your worth." Phil was my coach for two years and runs Life Strategies, LLC (www.coachinglifestrategies.com). These seven words landed on me in a powerful way, and I gobbled them up as a dose of daily wisdom.

And so, "Whatever happens is perfect" (WHIP) became our new mantra. Shout-out here to Lex Sisney, who captured this phrase before a family trip that we took to Vietnam that felt a bit stressful.

STEP 4: GET IN AND STAY IN YOUR GENIUS ZONE

Your zone of genius is your unique power. It is at the intersection of what you are uniquely talented at and where you get the most energy. I originally learned about the genius zone from my coach Lex Sisney. The first time I saw it published was in Gay Hendricks's book *The Big Leap* (New York, HarperCollins, 2010).

There is another model that I really like. Josh Steimle, in *The 7 Systems of Influence*, drafted a fun way of finding your genius zone. "How to Find Your Genius Zone," https://www.joshsteimle.com/influence/how-to-find-your-genius-zone.html.

STEP 5: TAKE ACTION

In fact, Tim Ferriss, the author of many books, including *Tools of Titans* and *The 4-Hour Workweek*, promotes a framework called fear-setting. "Fear-Setting: The Most Valuable Exercise I Do Every Month," May 2017, https://tim.blog/2017/05/15/fear-setting/.

I have a good friend, Andrew Sykes, who practices in the world of behavioral science and understanding why people do what they do. Andrew introduced me to the concept of hyperbolic discounting. You can learn more about Andrew at www.andrewsykes.com.

As a coach of mine once said, "If you're not at the table for a Win-4-All, it's not a Win-4-All." Shout-out here to Deb Katz, who is a coach through the Conscious Leadership Group. She made this comment when I shared my struggle with working to make everyone around me successful but not feeling successful myself.

Over time, my business partner, Eric Page, adapted something he calls the "six-step process to get what you want

out of life." There are a number of variations of the six-step process, but I like Eric's. As he always says, "Start with the goal, and don't jump to solutions until you have diagnosed the problems to achieving that goal." Right on!

The best way to affirm that is by repeating what we think we heard and then asking, "Is that right?" If they say, "Yes, that's right," then you can move on. I learned the technique of asking, "Is that right?" from the Black Swan Group. "The Seduction of 'You're Right' in Negotiations," March 2015, https://blog.blackswanltd.com/the-edge/2015/03/the-seduction-of-youre-right/.

But in that year, I had a conversation with a mentor who shared his approach to playing the game. The concept of "finish the game" was shared by Phil Dembo, who had provided mentorship to a number of professional athletes.